CALL in the CLOWNS

Children's Object Lessons

WESLEY T. RUNK

C.S.S. Publishing Co., Inc.
Lima, Ohio

CALL IN THE CLOWNS!

8868 / ISBN 1-55673-071-3

Table of Contents

Foreword

What child doesn't love to hear a story?

These short "parables-from-life" are based on Gospel Scripture texts, and are designed to be presented by the pastor or a worship leader, either at the worship service or at Sunday church school, vacation Bible school, or children's worship time. Each makes use of some common, everyday items.

None of the messages are intended to be presented just as they are written. In fact, none of us talk the way we write. The story-teller will want to read the Scripture text and the story (and if necessary rehearse it), until it can be presented in a natural story-telling way.

Often tellers of children's messages forget that they are speaking, *not to the adults* who also happen to be present (even though the adults properly are "overhearing" everything), but that first and primarily the message is a message *to the children* who are gathered in the chancel, or wherever the story is being told. The story-teller will want to be certain that the youngest child who comes to listen can understand what is being said. If eyes and hands begin to stray, make it simpler still, (and, perhaps, be prepared to depart from your "learned script" long enough to regain every youngster's attention).

Now, get ready to invite the youngsters, and to say, "Good morning, boys and girls . . ."

Your Name Is Important

Matthew 1:18-25, v. 21

She will bear a son, and you shall call his name Jesus, for he will save his people from their sins.

Object: A name chart with a list of names.

Good morning, boys and girls. Today we are going to talk about something that is very important to you. We are going to talk about your name and the names of others. All of you have names, don't you? [*Let them answer.*] Let's tell everyone your name. [*Encourage each of them to stand and speak his or her name.*] Names are very important. We not only call each other by a name, but we write our names on important papers. And when we get married we usually give our names, if we are a boy, to the girl that we marry or, if we are a girl, we usually take the name of our husband. There are a lot of things that we use our names for and that is what makes a name so important.

I have a list of names in this book that parents sometimes use when they are waiting for their baby to be born. Every name that you can think of is listed in this book and it also says what the name means. I picked some names out of the Bible to see what they meant and I will share them with you. Did you know that the name David means "beloved" or that Ruth means "companion"? Here is a good one, Philip means a "lover of horses" and, of course, Peter means "rock." Martha is another way of saying "lady" and the prophet Malachi was named to mean "my messenger." Those are just a few of the names in the Bible that have a special meaning to us.

But here is the most special one of all. Do you know what the name of Jesus means? Do you remember that an angel of God came and spoke to Joseph, and told him that Mary, the woman he loved, was going to have a baby boy? [*Let them answer*.] The angel also told Joseph what God wanted Joseph and Mary to name the baby. Did you remember that also? [*Let them answer*.] The angel told Joseph that God wanted this baby to be called Jesus. Do you know why God wanted them to call him Jesus? [*Let them answer*.] Because, the name Jesus means "to save God's people from their sins." That is what the name Jesus means. Your name means something: the name Philip means "lover of horses" and Jesus means "saving God's people from their sins." That's what Jesus did. That is why the name of Jesus is so important and why God did not name him Pat or Henry or Bill or any other name. God wanted people to know Jesus and also to know what Jesus was going to do. Now you know why names are so very important and why Jesus' name is the most important of all.

Grow Like a Fruit Tree

Matthew 3:1-12, v. 10

*Even now the axe is laid to the root of the trees; every tree
therefore that does not bear good fruit is cut down and thrown
into the fire.*

Object: An axe.

Good morning, boys and girls. I have with me this morning a tool that not many of you have used. It is a dangerous
tool and you must be very careful when you use it. I am sure
that you have seen your father or someone else use it when
he had a certain kind of job to do that needed chopping. We
call it an axe. How many of you know what you might chop
with an axe? [*Let them answer.*] That's right, you can chop
up firewood. You can also chop down a tree, make stakes for
your tent, or, if you wanted to, you could build a log cabin
as people used to do. There are a lot of ways to use an axe,
but the most important use for an axe is to chop down and
get rid of things that you want to get rid of around your home
or work.

Jesus once talked about using an axe when he was telling
a parable. A parable is a story that teaches us something. Jesus
said that when fruit trees stop making fruit we should get rid
of them. Chop them down and use them for firewood or
whatever you need the wood for. There is no sense letting a
fruit tree that is not making good fruit stand and take up space
where another fruit tree could grow. That sounds right and
I am sure that all of us agree with Jesus.

But Jesus told that story with a teaching because he wanted
us to learn something about ourselves and the way that we belong to God. We are like fruit trees, Jesus said, and that means
that we are supposed to grow fruit like trees do. Of course,
we can't actually grow fruit. Do you know anyone who grows

apples or pears or oranges at the ends of their fingers or el-
bows? [*Let them answer.*] I don't either. But we are expected
to grow in our love and our forgiving others who may have
hurt us. We should grow in believing that Jesus is the Son of
God and our Savior. We should believe those things more today than we did yesterday, and that is growing. We should
grow in sharing our money and our time with people who need
them. Now if we are not growing, then Jesus says that we could
be like the fruit tree that does not grow any fruit. That tree
is taken away or cut down so that another tree can grow in
its place.

You don't want anyone to take your place with Jesus do
you? [*Let them answer.*] Good, I don't want you to lose your
place either, so we must grow up in our belief that Jesus is
our God and that we are going to share him with the whole
world.

The Constitution of Our Faith

Matthew 5:1-12, v. 2

And he opened his mouth and taught them, saying:

Object: A constitution (United States, state or local government). Slips of paper for each child with Matthew 5:1-12 written on them.

Good morning, boys and girls. Today we are going to talk about something that you may have heard about a lot of times but perhaps you have never seen. How many of you have heard the word "constitution"? [*Let them answer.*] That's good. How many of you know what a constitution is? [*Let them answer.*] You have some good ideas. A constitution is something that people write for their organization to tell how it should be run and what they believe in. I have a copy of the United States Constitution that tells how our government should be set up and what we believe in as Americans. This is a great constitution, and it is something that we pay a lot of attention to every day of our lives. There are other constitutions such as the one for our state, and we have one for our church. I can show you the one that we have for our church. Constitutions are important and a lot of thinking and planning goes into every one. If you follow the constitution of your country, your church, or your club, then you will be a better citizen, church person, or club member.

Jesus gave the Christian church a kind of constitution one day when he was teaching his disciples and a lot of other people what it meant to be a follower of God. The words that he taught are thought to be some of the most important words that have ever been spoken by anyone to someone else. I cannot think of any words that are more important, because these tell me exactly what a Christian is supposed to be like, according to Jesus. I am not going to read the words to you today, but I am going to tell you where you can find them in the Bible, and I hope your mother and father will sit down with you today and go over them.

Each of the words that Jesus used was carefully chosen, and it teaches us the importance of love and how we are to use the love that God gives to us. It tells us how to care for each other and how God cares for us. These verses are called the Beatitudes, but they could be called the Constitution of our Faith. I hope that you will spend some time today reading the Bible with your parents and listening to the words that Jesus taught us about how to live. How many of you will do that? That's good.

Jesus' Job Description

Matthew 11:2-11, vv. 4-5

*And Jesus answered them, "Go and tell John what you hear
and see: the blind receive their sight and the lame walk, lepers
are cleansed and the deaf hear, and the dead are raised up,
and the poor have good news preached to them."*

*Objects: A blackboard, some chalk, and some ideas on the job description
of a mother.*

Good morning, boys and girls. Have you all been busy since
I saw you last week? I know I've been busy. Sometimes it seems
like adults are always busy, doesn't it? I think some of the
busiest people are mothers. I thought that we might make a
list of some of the things that your mother does, and then we
can all see how busy she is. You tell me what your mother does
for you and I will make a list on the chalkboard. [*Invite some
responses and prod where necessary with some things that they
may not think about.*]

That is quite a list. And we have forgotten a lot of the things
that a mother does every day. I know this, if I showed this
list of things to someone who was not here this morning they
would guess right away that we were talking about a mother's
job.

Now I am going to give you another list and I want you
to tell me who you think this job belongs to. This person makes
the blind see, the crippled walk; he heals the very sick and can
make deaf people hear. This person can even make the dead
come back to life and, finally, he takes care of the poor and
gives them hope with which to live. Do you know who can
do all of this and even more? [*Let them answer.*]

That's right, this was the job that Jesus was sent to do.
That is the work of the Savior, and no one else in the whole
world can do that job but he. No doctor or preacher or father

or mother, or anyone else can do it. Just the Savior.

A long time ago John the Baptizer sent his disciples to Jesus and asked him if he was the one that everyone was waiting for or if they should look for another. Jesus told them just what I told you. He told the disciples of John to look around and see what was happening and that this was the work of the Savior. Then he told them to go back to John and tell him what they saw.

Each of us has something that we are supposed to do, just as our mothers do all of the things that only a mother can do. But the job of Jesus is a very special one, and we call his work the work of the Savior. The next time someone asks you about Jesus' work, you can tell them the things that he does that no one else can do.

When Is Jesus Coming Back?

Matthew 24:37-44, v. 44

Therefore you also must be ready; for the Son of man is coming at an hour you do not expect.

Objects: An egg timer, a clock, and a television schedule.

Good morning, boys and girls. Did you know that Jesus Christ is coming back to earth? [*Let them answer.*] That's what the Bible says. It teaches us that Jesus is coming back at a certain time and that only the Father in heaven knows just when.

We know the time of almost everything we do, or want to do in the future. If I wanted to cook some eggs and make sure that they were just right, I would use this egg timer, set it for just the right time, and then wait for the timer to go off. If I want a three-minute egg, I turn the egg timer just the right number of times, and it will make sure that my eggs are perfect.

I can do the same thing with a clock. Let's suppose that I want to get up in the morning at 7:15. I set the alarm on the clock and go to sleep knowing that the alarm will go off and wake me up at 7:15.

I can also know when my favorite TV show is going to be on the air by looking at the TV schedule and finding the hour of the day that it is going to be on. I will not miss it by a minute.

But, now, let's suppose that I want to know when Jesus is coming back to earth. People have waited for a long time to see Jesus again, but it has not happened. I could tell you that it is going to happen tomorrow, but I don't really know when he is coming back. You could read the Bible from cover to cover and you would not know the time that Jesus is coming back. You can ask your mom or dad or any of your friends, but as much as they want to know themselves, they do not know. God has a reason for not telling us when he is coming back. He wants us to always be expecting him and to live like he were coming back today.

If you thought that Jesus were coming to your house to live this afternoon, would you not get ready for Jesus in a special way? Would you live a little differently if you knew that Jesus was going to meet you in your living room today? I know that you would, and it is for this reason that God is not telling us when he is coming. He is asking us to live every day like he was coming today.

You may know when you are getting up, how you like your eggs, and when your favorite TV show is on the air, but you will never know when Jesus is coming until the day and the moment he arrives.

Soft Blankets for a Baby
[Appropriate for use at Christmas]

Luke 2:1-20, v. 12

"And this will be a sign for you: you will find a babe wrapped in swaddling cloths and lying in a manger."

Objects: Receiving blankets for a baby.

Happy birthday, Jesus! Would you all like to sing happy birthday to Jesus? [*Lead them in a chorus of Happy Birthday.*] Does anyone know on what day we celebrate Jesus' birthday? [*Let them answer.*] That's right, on Christmas day. Of course, nobody knows when Jesus' birthday really is but that is when most of us celebrate it. I love Christmas and all of the things that it means to me. I am sure that all of you love it too. Is there anyone who does not like Christmas? [*Let them answer.*] I didn't think so, but I thought I would ask.

I have some very soft cloth with me today, and I wonder if you know what it is used for? [*Let them answer.*] Have any of you ever held a tiny baby in a cloth or blanket like this? That's good, I am glad that all of you have held a tiny baby, because I think it is one of the nicest things to hold in the world. When you see a blanket like this you must know that somewhere there is a baby who belongs to it.

An angel of God appeared to the shepherds and told them to go to Bethlehem and find a stable where there was a new baby born in a manger. The baby was going to be wrapped in a soft cloth like the one that you are touching. A baby was usually born in a house in those days, and very seldom, if ever, was a baby born in a stable. The angel told them to go and find a baby born in a stable that was wrapped in soft cloth, and when they did they would also find the Savior, Jesus Christ. Can you imagine how excited the shepherds must have felt? I know they were excited. First of all, I am sure that it was the first time that they had ever seen an angel. People usually don't see angels. Secondly, they were told to go and find a baby wrapped in a soft blanket that was lying in a manger. You know that a manger is something that animals eat out of, and that it was not a baby bed. So the shepherds knew that they were going to see something very unusual. But the angel wanted them to look for something unusual, because Jesus was not an ordinary baby. He was the Son of God and he was meant to save the world. The angel said that this was the sign. Of course, the shepherds did what they were told, and they went to Bethlehem and found a baby lying in a manger wrapped in soft cloth. That baby was Jesus, and Jesus is our Lord.

Maybe the next time that you see some soft blankets like this or when you see a baby wrapped up in them, you will think about the shepherds and how they found Jesus on that first Christmas day.

Save the Good Part

Luke 3:15-17, 21-22, v. 17

His winnowing fork is in his hand, to clear his threshing floor, and to gather the wheat into his granary, but the chaff he will burn with unquenchable fire.

Object: A banana.

Good morning, boys and girls. How many of you like bananas? [*Let them answer.*] A banana is one of my favorite fruits. I like to eat it on cereal, or I like to eat it all by itself. I guess my favorite way to eat a banana is in a banana split, but then I don't have those often. I brought a banana along today to see if you eat it the same way I do. Is there anyone here who would like to eat the banana for us? Let's all watch very carefully to see how she does it. [*Watch her for a moment until it is apparent that she is not going to eat the peeling.*] What are you going to do with the peeling? Does that mean that you are not going to eat it? [*Let her answer.*] Are you going to throw it away? [*You may act a little shocked.*] In other words you are only going to eat the inside of the banana, and you are going to throw the peeling in the garbage or do something to get rid of it. [*Let her answer.*] Is that the way the rest of you would eat a banana? [*Let them answer.*]

All right, I think that everyone knows that we do not eat banana peelings, because they are not good to eat. They are bitter, not tasty, and so we get rid of them.

The Bible says something like this when it talks about the way that God works with the people who obey him and the ones who do not. The Bible teaches us that, after our lives are lived here on earth, God makes a choice between the people who do obey him, and those who don't. The ones who obey him, love him, and live the way he teaches, are forgiven for any wrong that they do, and are asked to share his life in heaven. The ones who are wrong, have hate in their hearts, and are unforgiving, are done away with about the same way that you get rid of a banana peeling. There is no place for them in heaven.

I don't want to scare you. You should not be scared, but instead, you should be pleased to know that God wants to share his life with you. People who love God, and there are many, are going to have a wonderful life on earth and forever after with God in his heaven. That is what the Bible teaches, and it is what we believe. But if you want to know what happens to the people who do not love God, who hate what he teaches, then you can remember the way we care for a banana peel and you will have the answer. So the next time you eat a banana, I want you to remember that there is a good part and a bad part, and that the two parts are the two kinds of people who live in this world and how both of them know God.

It's Tempting

Luke 4:1-13, v. 12

And Jesus answered him, "It is said, 'You shall not tempt the Lord your God.' "

Object: A television schedule.

Good morning, boys and girls. I brought something along with me this morning that I think all of you will recognize immediately. [*Hold up the television guide.*] What is it? [*Let them answer.*] Right, it is the TV guide from the Saturday paper. If you want to know what is going to be on this week, or what the special programs are going to be for each day, you can read all about them in the TV guide. How many of you like TV? [*Let them answer.*] Do you watch it often? Do you wish that you could watch it more? [*Let them answer.*] How many of you think that you watch television too much? [*Let them answer.*] Not many of you think that you watch it too much. How many of your parents think that you watch it too much? [*Let them answer.*] I thought so.

If you had some homework to do and you also wanted to watch a special program on TV, which would you do? [*Let them answer.*] Does the TV ever tempt you to lie? [*Let them answer.*] I know some boys and girls who tell their mothers and dads that they don't have any homework, so that their parents will let them watch the TV. Anything we like as much as TV is bound to be a temptation. It causes us to act differently than we should, and say things that we should not, because we like TV so much that we do not want to give it up for anything.

We call that temptation. Jesus knew about temptation. As a matter of fact, he told the Devil one day that he should not tempt God or ask anyone else to tempt God. Temptation is a bad thing. The Devil tried to get Jesus to tempt God by asking

Jesus to jump off a high building, so that the angels would catch him before he hit the ground. Jesus said that there was no reason for him to jump off a high building. If you jumped from a high building, you would be hurt. If you do not study, but watch TV instead, you could flunk your school tests. We can't blame the TV. We have to blame ourselves instead. God says that we should not tempt ourselves or other people. When you do the wrong thing, you should not expect it to turn out right. We know how to act for God and with God, and when we don't do what we should, we have problems. When we do right and share our lives in the right way, we have right things happen to us.

Maybe the next time you decide to watch TV instead of doing your homework, you will remember how Jesus told the Devil to leave when he tried to get Jesus to tempt God. Then you will turn off the TV and do what is expected of you. The TV can be good, or it can be a temptation for you. Only you know when it is right and when it is wrong. Use it the right way and you will be pleasing to God and to yourself.

A Good Custom

Luke 4:14-21, v. 16

And he came to Nazareth, where he had been brought up; and he went to the synagogue, as his custom was, on the sabbath day.

Objects: *Praying hands and bowed head.*

Good morning, boys and girls. How many of you know what a custom is or what I mean by the word "custom"? [*Let them answer.*] A custom is something that you do at a particular time. You always do it no matter how many times it happens. Putting up the Christmas tree is a custom in most homes at Christmas time. Even when there are no children at home, people still have a Christmas tree in their house. It may be large or small, but they have a tree.

Praying is a custom. I pray before every meal. I am sure that most of you pray before you eat, to thank God for the food and all of the good things he has done for you. You probably also pray before you fall asleep at night and when you get up in the morning. It is good to talk to God and to share all of your thoughts with him. It is a custom to pray. We even make it more of a custom when we fold our hands like this, and then bow our heads in this way. [*Demonstrate the posture of prayer.*] It is a custom, and a wonderful custom, and it has been done by people and families for thousands of years. If you don't do it, I hope you will begin today.

Jesus prayed. It was a custom of Jesus to pray, and he also had other customs which I would like to share with you. The one custom that the Bible tells us about this morning is the custom that Jesus had of going to church on the day of worship. The Bible tells us that it was his custom to go every week to worship God. Isn't that wonderful? Jesus did the same thing that you and I do. He did not think that he was so good that he didn't have to go to church. As a matter of fact, Jesus loved to go to worship and be with all of his friends and family, and sing the Psalms, and read the Scriptures. The story we hear today is that when he went back home to the church where he was raised, he also went to church with his neighbors, and read the Scriptures, and preached to the people about who he was.

You don't have to preach, but I am sure that it is good when you take your turn in Sunday church school and help to read from the Bible, and share your prayers with your friends. It is a good custom to pray, and also to attend church every Sunday in the same way that Jesus followed his custom and prayed and went to church. I hope you remember the word "custom" and that you will make it a custom to come to church every Sunday.

Jesus in the News

Luke 4:21-30, v. 23

And he said to them, "Doubtless you will quote to me this proverb, 'Physician, heal yourself; what we have heard you did at Capernaum, do here also in your own country.' "

Object: A newspaper.

Good morning, boys and girls. How many of you have read the newspaper that was delivered to your house yesterday? [*Let them answer.*] Tell me what you have read. [*Let them answer.*] You read the funnies and what else? [*Let them answer.*] Most of you do not read the rest of the paper yet, but before long you will. When you do you will read about some very interesting people and the things that they have done. You also will read some interesting things about people who live in other towns and cities. When someone does something that is very interesting in another city, the newspaper prints it in our town and we read about the things that person has done. [*Read such an article in the newspaper that you brought with you.*]

This is the way that it was with Jesus. When Jesus came into a town, the people had already heard about the things that he had done in other places. They wanted him to do the same things for them. The news traveled fast.

But Jesus was not just doing things so that people could write about him in the newspaper, or talk about him to friends and neighbors. That was not the reason. Jesus did what he wanted to do for people who were ill because they were ill, and because they believed in the power of God to make them well. Jesus called that kind of belief "faith."

When Jesus came to his home town, the people did not believe that he was the Son of God. Instead, they thought that he was just like all of the other boys who had grown up there, but with some special magic. They knew him as the son of

Mary and Joseph, and not as the Son of God. They did not have faith or believe that God wanted to make them well. Because the people did not believe Jesus, he could not cure them. He could not cure someone who did not believe that it was God who was doing the healing.

We have read a lot about Jesus and talked a lot about Jesus. You can find something in your newspaper almost every day about him. If you do not believe that his power comes from God, then Jesus is not something special to you. Reading about him, or talking about him, doesn't make him the Savior. Believing in him does, and that is what the people of Nazareth did not do.

We want to believe in Jesus and believe that he can do what he says, so we must have faith that Jesus is the Son of God with great power. When you read about him in your newspaper, then you can say that you also know him in your heart. God bless You.

Strange Fishing

Luke 5:1-11, v. 10b

And Jesus said to Simon, "Do not be afraid; henceforth you will be catching men."

Object: A badminton net.

Good morning, boys and girls. I read in the Bible today that Jesus said he was going to make men like Peter and John fishers of men. Do you know what that means? [*Let them answer.*] I think it means that they would catch men just like they caught fish. Did you know that Peter and his brother Andrew, and also James and John were fishermen? That was their job and they were pretty good at it. Every morning they would get in their boats and go out on the lake to catch fish and bring them home to sell. Some days they would catch a lot, and some days they would catch very few. There are not many people who still fish the way they did in those days. But can you imagine catching men in a net like you catch fish? Do you think that this is what Jesus meant when he said that he would make them fishers of men? [*Let them answer.*] Let's suppose that this is what he meant. I have a big net here and I am going to catch some boys and girls. [*Take the net and throw it over the children.*] Now, what do I do with you? I don't think this is what Jesus meant when he talked about being fishers of men.

What Jesus did mean was that he was going to teach the disciples about God's love, so that they could teach other people. Jesus wanted the disciples to learn as much as they could from him so that, when they began teaching the people about God, those people would also become disciples of Jesus. That is what Jesus meant when he talked about catching men. He didn't want to catch people in a net. He wanted to make them disciples. But he knew that Peter and John would understand him better if he told them that they were going to stop catching fish and instead start "catching" people.

Jesus would like to make you fishers of people also. He wants all of his disciples to look for ways to teach people about the wonderful things that God can do for us. If people are going to learn about God, they must first be "caught," or spoken to, by other people like you and me.

Maybe the next time you see a big net, you will remember the time that Jesus told Peter how he was going to make him a fisher of men, and what that really means. I hope you remember also to be a fisher and to teach someone about the good things that God does for you.

Jesus the Healer

Luke 6:17-26, v. 19

*And all the crowd sought to touch him, for power came forth
from him and healed them all.*

Object: A heating pad.

Good morning, boys and girls. How many of you have ever
used a heating pad? [*Let them answer.*] When do you like to
use it the most? [*Let them answer.*] Those are all good times,
but I suppose that the best time for all of us to use the heating
pad is when we do not feel too well. If we have an earache
or a backache, or any kind of an ache, it is always good to
use the heating pad. There is that nice warm feeling that seems
to make us feel better.

I want you to feel my heating pad and then tell me what
caused it to make me feel better. [*Pass the heating pad among
the children.*] What is it that gives this heating pad the power
to make me feel better? [*Let them answer.*] That's right, it is
electricity. The power to make that pad hot comes from the
cord that is plugged into the wall. The electricity comes through
wires, and the wires go all the way back to a big plant somewhere that makes electricity out of coal, water, or something
else. There is a great power in electricity, and it is used for
many things, but one of the things we use electricity for is a
heating pad. And the reason that we use the heating pad is
to make our bumps, bruises, and aches feel better.

Jesus must have been like a heating pad. People got better
just by touching him. The Bible tells us today about the time
when people stood in line, or all around him, just to try to
touch him so that they would feel better. And you know what?
They did feel better. The Bible tells us that Jesus was able to
cure people of bad diseases when all he did was touch them
or they touched him.

Of course the power did not come from coal, water, or anything like that. It wasn't even electricity. The power that Jesus had to cure people came from God, and I guess you could call it a kind of healing love. God gave Jesus a special power to make people who were sick well again. But people could feel the power coming through Jesus, just like you and I can feel the heat coming through the heating pad.

Maybe the next time you use a heating pad, you will think of the power that comes from the electricity, and when you do that, you will also remember the special power that God gave to Jesus to heal people who were sick.

A Dog Named Sport

Luke 7:1-10, v. 7

Therefore I did not presume to come to you. But say the word, and let my servant be healed.

Object: An invisible dog named Sport.

Good morning, boys and girls. I brought along with me this morning a friend who is invisible. Sport just loves to come to church, and being an invisible dog, he comes quite often. But he is kind of shy, and I only use him in children's sermons once in a while. Sport is a beautiful dog. What color would you say he is? [*Let them answer, and whatever color they give, he can be. They can also describe him as a dog with short ears, long ears, tall, short, or whatever they want him to be.*] I told you he was a beautiful invisible dog. I want to let you each pet him once, and then I am going to have him go over and sit down for a moment. [*Let them each pet him and then send him to a certain spot.*] The thing I like most about Sport is that he will do whatever I say. [*Tell Sport to do some tricks and compliment him on his obedience.*] Thank you, Sport.

Now the reason that I brought Sport with me this morning was to help me tell you another story that we find in the Bible. It is the story about a time when Jesus was asked to come to the home of a soldier. He was not a private, but he wasn't a general either. This soldier had a man who worked for him who was very sick. The soldier loved this man and wanted him to be well more than almost anything else. He heard about Jesus, and he sent some friends to ask Jesus if he would come and heal the man. Jesus was so impressed about the soldier because of the nice things that other people said about him that he went immediately. Before Jesus arrived at the soldier's house there was someone sent to meet him and tell him that he did not have to come any farther. The soldier knew that whatever Jesus said, would be done. Jesus did not have to be in his house to make this man well. The soldier knew that Jesus could do the same thing with life that he could do with other things. When the soldier gave an order to one of his men, the man did it. When he gave an order he considered the job done. The soldier knew that if Jesus would only command that the man be healed, he would be healed.

This is a great lesson for all of us to learn. It is called "faith." The soldier knew that if Jesus wanted to heal the man, he would and could heal him. All Jesus had to do was to ask his Father in heaven to do it and it would be done.

That is the way Sport is with me. I tell him to do something, and I know that Sport will do it. Maybe the next time you think about my dog Sport you will remember the faith that I have in Sport to do anything that I ask him to do, and when you think of that, then you will also think about what our faith in God means, and how much we must trust him to have all things done.

Compassion

Luke 7:11-17, v. 13

*And when the Lord saw her, he had compassion on her and
said to her, "Do not weep."*

Object: A nurse's cap.

Good morning, boys and girls. How many of you have ever
been hurt so badly that you had to go to the hospital to be
cared for by the doctors and nurses? [*Let them answer.*] Some
of you have been there. Do you remember how afraid you
were? [*Let them answer.*] First of all, you hurt pretty badly,
and second you were not sure what was going to happen to
you. That would make anyone afraid. Do you remember how
nice the nurses were to you that day and every day that you
were in the hospital? [*Let them answer.*] They were really something special and they made all of the worry and fear go right
out of you.

I brought along a nurse's cap with me this morning so that
you could think about nurses when I tell you a big word. The
word is "compassion," and that is what the nurses feel for
you when you come into the hospital. They have compassion
for you. That is another word, only a nice powerful word, for
caring. They not only feel strongly for you, but they also take
care of what is hurting you. And the nurses will be there to
keep taking care of you until you are well enough to go home.

Jesus was a person who was filled with compassion. He
had compassion for all who needed him, and that includes
everyone. I remember the story in the Bible about a woman
who was walking to the cemetery to bury her son. She had
already buried her husband after he died, and now she was
all alone. The people who walked with her were carrying the
body of her son, and they were all very sad. Jesus watched
the people coming towards him, and the Bible said that he had

compassion for her. That means that he not only felt sorry for her hurt, but that he was going to do something about it. First he told her not to cry any more, which is another way of telling her that she would soon have nothing to be sad about. Then he went over to the place where the body was being carried and told the son to wake up, to come back to life. And I am sure that you know what happened. The man who was dead was brought back to life.

That was just one sign of Jesus' compassion. Jesus has compassion on lots of people. He cares about us, and he does something about it. Nurses have compassion, and, when you see a cap like this, you can remember that the nurses, like many other people, learn their compassion from God. We should all have compassion, which means that when we see someone who needs us, we should care and do what we can to help them.

Learning to Forgive a Lot

Luke 7:36-50, v. 47

*Therefore I tell you, her sins, which are many, are forgiven,
for she loved much; but he who is forgiven little, loves little.*

Object: *A small bag of potatoes and a twenty-pound bag of potatoes.*

Good morning, boys and girls. Today we are going to have
a little experiment that I hope will prove something about the
way that God loves and takes care of us. I need two volun-
teers to help me this morning. [*Choose two, one of them a
lot smaller than the other if possible. We want to give the larger
sack of potatoes to the smaller child.*] Now the only thing that
you must do to help in this experiment is to each hold a sack
of potatoes. [*Hand out the sacks.*] Now I want you to hold
these sacks while I tell a story about Jesus.

A long time ago, Jesus ate dinner in the house of a very
important person. While he was there, a woman who did not
have a very good reputation showed up at the place where they
were eating, and began to pay a lot of attention to Jesus. She
washed his feet and dried them with her hair, and she did a
lot of other things that showed how much she believed in him
as someone special. The people who were eating were shocked
that Jesus would let someone with such great sin care for him.
They said some pretty nasty things to Jesus, and about the
lady. Of course, she could hear what they said, but they never
talked to her and, instead, just pretended that she was not there
as a person, but only as a bad thing.

Jesus then said to the important man that he had done none
of the things for him that she had done, even though he was
a guest in his house. It was true that she had sinned a lot, and
it would take a lot of forgiveness to forgive her. But Jesus said
that when you forgive a person a lot, then they also love a lot.

I want to prove that last point. I am going to take away

the potatoes from this person and see if he is really glad that I have taken them away. [*Take away the potatoes from the large child with the small bag.*] Do you feel really happy that I have taken away the potatoes so that you do not have to carry them any longer? [*Now take away the big sack from the little person.*] How do you feel now that I have helped you? [*Let this one answer.*] You seem a lot happier than the other person. Do you think it's because you had the bigger sack? [*Let them answer.*] I think that this has something to do with it.

I think that this is what Jesus was trying to tell the people that day. The woman knew that she had sinned a lot. She was so glad for the forgiveness of Jesus that she wanted to do something to show it. The others felt that they had not done much wrong, and therefore they did not appreciate what Jesus did for them. It is a hard lesson to learn, but an important one to know that the forgiveness of Jesus is the most precious gift we have.

Eric Eraser

Luke 9:18-24, v. 24

For whoever would save his life will lose it; and whoever loses his life for my sake, he will save it.

Object: A well-worn rubber eraser.

Good morning, boys and girls. Today we are going to talk about one of the teachings of Jesus that changed the world. It changed the way that people think and act. I brought along a little friend of mine to help me show you how important that teaching is. I hope that it will help you to think and act as Jesus taught us to. My friend's name is Eric. His whole name is Eric Eraser. How many of you have a friend who looks just like my friend Eric? [*Let them answer.*] Take a close look at Eric and you will see that he is not the same as he used to be. [*Show them the well-worn rubber eraser.*] Does he look kind of worn out and used up? [*Let them answer.*] He is. That's the way that Eric likes it. Eric would not have it any other way. The best thing that can happen to Eric is for me to use him to correct one of my many mistakes.

I guess there are some erasers that would like to stay neat and clean and never be used. But that is not the way that Eric feels. Eric knows that the only way he knows that he is alive is to be used, and that is the way that he wants to live. I want you to know that this is the way that Jesus taught us to live.

Some people always want to save themselves, just like some erasers. They never want to be used, and so they never live. They just lie in a box somewhere and are completely forgotten. But live erasers are ones that are used every day for every mistake until they are all gone. They love life and can hardly wait until they are all used up.

Every Christian should feel this way about the special promise made to us by Jesus. Jesus promises us that when we use up this life by living it the way that he teaches us to live, he will give us a new life that is even better than the one that we have now.

That is why I want all of you to be like Eric. He is not all used up yet, just like many Christians are not used up yet, but when he is used up, he will be happy. You will be happy, too, if you live for Jesus and share your life in love with all of God's people.

That is the story of Eric Eraser, and I hope you remember it today and every day, as you share the things that Jesus taught you with your friends and all of the people that you meet. Will you do that? Good. God Bless You.

What a Change!

Luke 9:28-36, v. 29

*And as he was praying, the appearance of his countenance was
altered, and his raiment became dazzling white.*

Object: A very dusty mirror and some glass cleaner.

Good morning, boys and girls. Things have a way of changing, don't they? The weather changes, the time changes, we
change our clothes and our friends and almost everything else
that we can think of around us. Can you think of one thing
that does not change? [*Let them answer.*] I guess the only thing
that I can think of that does not change is God's love.

I want to tell you about a time that Jesus changed and some
of the disciples saw it happen. They were with him when this
change took place, and they watched Jesus become dazzling
white. That is the way that the Bible described Jesus when he
made this change.

I brought along a mirror of mine to help you see what I
mean when I talk about something changing. This mirror is
pretty dusty and clouded. You can see yourself in it, but if
you had your choice, you would want it different. Most of
the time we do not even notice a mirror when it is dusty, but
let me show you what happens when we clean it. [*Proceed to
clean the mirror and make the glass shine.*] Now you can really
tell the difference between the way that it was and the way
that it is now. The mirror has changed.

Jesus changed from his normal-looking self to a dazzling
white. It happened one day when Jesus took Peter, James, and
John up a mountain to pray, and to be alone with God. While
they were there, they had a very strange experience not only
of Jesus changing, but also of being visited by some men who
had died thousands of years ago. Right there, where they stood,
appeared Moses and Elijah. Peter was so excited that he could

hardly speak. And then to make it complete, as one of the most unusual days in the disciples' lives, they heard the voice of God saying, "This is my Son, my Chosen; listen to him." You can imagine how impressed Peter, James, and John were when they saw what they saw and heard what they heard. They knew for certain that Jesus was something special, not only to them, but to the Father in heaven.

Maybe the next time you are standing in front of a mirror, or maybe when you watch someone clean a mirror, you will remember the day that Jesus changed. It was an important day for Jesus, and an important day for everyone who believes in Jesus.

Hoe Jesus' Row

Luke 9:51-62, v. 62

*Jesus said to him, "No one who puts his hand to the plow
and looks back is fit for the kingdom of God."*

Object: *A garden hoe.*

Good morning, boys and girls. Today we are going to learn
something about farming or having a garden, and while we
are doing this, we hope to learn something about the kingdom of God. Let's see if we can do this.

I brought a hoe with me this morning. How many of you
have ever used a hoe? [*Let them answer.*] If you have used
one, then tell me how to use it. [*Let someone explain or demonstrate the way that he or she uses it.*] You must be a very good
farmer. If you use a hoe like this, you should not have any
weeds in your garden, and your plants should be growing very
well. Sometimes you must use a hoe to plant a garden, and
that means having straight rows. Have you ever seen someone try to make a straight row with a hoe? [*Let them answer.*]
I am going to show you two ways to use a hoe, and I want
you to tell me which way is the best way to have a straight
row. [*Demonstrate lining up the hoe with a supposed marker
straight ahead, and then hoe by looking back over your shoulder. As you walk, you should make it fairly obvious that looking over your shoulder produces a crooked path.*] Which way
seems best to you? [*Let them answer.*] That's right, the best
way is to look straight ahead so that you know where you have
been, if you want to keep on going in a straight line. If you
look over your shoulder, you will make a crooked path.

The same thing is true about being a member of God's kingdom. Jesus knew that there were some people who wanted to
be a part of the group who believed in Jesus, but that they
also wanted things to be like they used to be for them. In other

words, they liked what Jesus said and did, and hoped that it would happen to them, but they did not want to give up some of their sins. They always wanted to be able to go back and do the things that they used to do, like telling a lie if they needed to, instead of telling the truth. Jesus said you can't be a part of God's world one day and wish you were part of the other way another day. That won't work. You can't have it both ways. It is like hoeing your garden and looking over your shoulder; you never get to the place that you want to be, and instead you always get somewhere where you don't want to be. If you make up your mind that you want to be a Christian, then you must forget about the other things, and just keep looking forward to the time when you shall be with God in God's world.

Yummy Good Spinach

Luke 10:1-9, v. 8

Whenever you enter a town and they receive you, eat what is set before you.

Object: *A package of spinach.*

Good morning, boys and girls. I hope that all of you love spinach, because that is what I want to share with you today. How many of you just love spinach? [*Let them answer.*] None of you like spinach? Isn't there someone here who would like it if I put some vinegar on it with salt and pepper? None of you like vinegar? Suppose I invited you to my house and I served you spinach on your plate, and I just expected you to eat it. What would you do? [*Let them answer.*] Would you make faces and not eat it if you knew that it would hurt my feelings? [*Let them answer.*]

I had to ask you these questions because Jesus told his disciples a lot of things when he sent them out to teach others about Christianity, and one of the things that he told them was to eat whatever the people offered them in their homes. Jesus told them that it was very important to have good manners about what they ate and how they lived, so that people would not have an excuse not to like them. Jesus did not care what it was that the people offered his disciples to eat while they stayed in their homes. They were supposed to eat it and be thankful for it. Do you think that you could have been one of the disciples of Jesus? [*Let them answer.*] Why do you think that Jesus told them to act this way? [*Let them answer.*]

People think that what they eat is what all people eat, and they also think that it is very good. If you tell them that you don't like what they serve for food, then the people also think that you don't like them. If you came to tell me about Jesus and to show me how much you love him, and I gave you spinach to eat, and you said you didn't like the spinach, then I might think more about the spinach, and how you don't like the way that I cook it, than I do about what you are trying to tell me about Jesus. Does that make sense to you? [*Let them answer.*]

Having good manners is always important. I am not just talking about when you are teaching about Jesus. But it is very important that you do not make people feel bad about other things when you are trying to teach them about Jesus.

The next time that you are a guest at someone's house and they share their food with you, I want you to remember this and how Jesus taught his disciples to be polite and never make someone feel bad toward you. That is something that all Christians must learn if they are going to teach the whole world about Jesus.

You Need All the Pieces

Luke 10:25-37, v. 27

And he answered, "You shall love the Lord your God with all your heart, and with all your soul, and with all your strength, and with all your mind; and your neighbor as yourself."

Object: *A jigsaw puzzle.*

Good morning, boys and girls. How many of you know what the word "all" means? [*Let them answer.*] Is it an important word? [*Let them answer.*] The word "all" means a lot and it is a very important word. Sometimes if you don't have it all, you don't have anything. Let me show you what I mean. I brought along a jigsaw puzzle. It has a lot of pieces and it will take all of the pieces to make the whole puzzle. If one of the pieces is missing, the puzzle is ruined, and you cannot have a whole picture. I want you to know that there is one piece of the puzzle missing. Isn't that awful? [*Let them answer.*]

This is the way Jesus felt about the way that people should feel about God. When someone asked him how they should be toward God, he asked them what the Bible said. They knew what the Bible said, and so they repeated the words that they had heard so often. The Bible says that you should love God with all of your heart, all of your soul, all of your mind, and all of your strength. It did not say part of your mind or part of your soul or part of your heart or part of your strength. It just isn't like that. You have to give God "all" that you have if you want to give him anything.

Loving God is like making a puzzle. You have to do it all, you have to give it all, because that is the way that God wants it. Part of a puzzle is not good enough. If you put it all together and you were missing one part, you would search and search until you found the one piece that was missing, and then you would put it in and be very happy.

That is the way it is with loving God. If you are saving some of your love for something else instead of giving it to God, you will find that you are always looking for the part that you have not given him. You are looking and looking and looking for whatever is missing and keeping you from loving God. But, when you find what you have been hiding even from yourself, and you give it to God, then you are really happy. Give all of your love to God and you will know why Jesus taught us to do what he wanted us to do. The word "all" is a very important word, and, if you do not believe me, then hide one piece of the next puzzle that you do and see how much you miss it. Find that piece and put it together, and then you will know why it is important to love God with all that you have to share.

Do You Choose Marge or Chris?

Luke 10:38-42, v. 42a

Mary has chosen the good portion, which shall not be taken away from her.

Object: A candy bar and a glass of milk.

Good morning, boys and girls. Today we are going to talk about the way that people spend their time with Jesus. It is a good lesson and one that all of us should learn. Sometimes we have to learn this lesson over and over again. I brought along some friends of yours that I am sure all of you like. I have with me Marge Milk and Chris Candy Bar. Both of them are good, and, if I told you that you could have as much as you wanted of one or the other, I am sure that you would choose both of them. But if I told you that you could have only one of them, and the one that you chose would be the one that you would have for the rest of your life, I wonder which one you would choose. Let me see your hands, and then I will know which one you like the most. [*Let them vote for one or the other.*] Some of you have chosen the milk, but most of you have chosen the candy bar. I wonder which was the good choice. The one is going to build you into a strong boy or girl, while the other one is going to give you cavities if you eat too much of it. Do you know which one is which? That's right, the candy bar is not really good if you have too much, but the milk is good for you no matter how much you drink. We have to make choices all of the time and our choices are important.

Today we find that Jesus was asked to settle an argument between two sisters. One of the sisters felt like she wanted to have a clean house and serve a good dinner, while the other sister wanted to know all that she could learn from Jesus.

Having a clean house is important, and cooking good meals is important, but I wonder which is the most important. If you had your choice between listening to Jesus and serving him a good meal, which one would you take? Both of them thought that they were making the right choice. But Jesus said that the sister who learned was making the right choice. Spending time learning and loving God is the most important choice, and it should come above everything else. The rest of the things that we do or have to do should come after our loving and learning about God.

Some people put working around the church ahead of worshiping God. They think that they are serving God, but really they are serving themselves. Jesus said it is better to worship and share our lives with him than it is to do anything else. It is a hard lesson to learn, and one that we must learn many times; but it is a good lesson, and one that we should never forget.

Snakes on Your Plate

Luke 11:1-13, vv. 11-12

What father among you, if his son asks for a fish, will instead of a fish give him a serpent; or if he asks for an egg, will give him a scorpion?

Objects: *A plastic, or rubber, snake and spider.*

Good morning, boys and girls. How many of you like snakes and spiders? [*Let them answer.*] Some of you like them, but alot of you don't like them. The older they get, the less most people like them. I don't know many people who like snakes when they grow older, but when we are young, we do seem to like the things that crawl and slither in the grass.

But now I have another question for you. How would you like to come to dinner or breakfast and ask for an egg or a fish, and, when your mother brought you your food, see a snake or a big spider on your plate instead of the fish or egg? [*Let them answer.*] Can you imagine having a plate full of snakes or spiders? [*Let them answer.*] I can't either. Do you think that your mother or father would give you snakes and spiders if you asked for a fish or an egg? [*Let them answer.*] Fathers and mothers are not like this. We trust our mothers and fathers to give us what we need, and they would never trick us by giving us something that could harm us or scare us.

Jesus told us that our Father in heaven is a lot like our mother and father on earth are in this way. God is not going to trick us with something that would be bad for us or scare us in a terrible way. If we ask for love, he will give us love, and not hate. If we are wanting help, he will give us help, and he will not trick us with something else. Jesus says that we can trust God to give us whatever we need, when we need it.

You would never expect your father or mother to scare you or break a promise to you. Parents are not like that to their children. When they promise something they keep the promise. God is like that also because he never breaks a promise. Of course, we must ask him for the things that we want. We can't just wait and hope that God gives us everything. God wants us to ask for the things that we need, so that he can decide how to give them.

Jesus compared our parents to the Father in Heaven often, because they act a lot like the way that God acts toward us. But I want you to know that God loves us even more than our parents, and that means that he loves us a bunch. The next time that you have something to eat, and you know your mom did not give you a snake or spider, I want you to think about the way God wants to share his life with all of us and answer all of our prayers.

What Do You Do with the Left-Over Jelly Beans?

Luke 12:13-21, v. 17

*And he thought to himself, "What shall I do, for I have no-
where to store my crops?"*

Object: A large bag of jelly beans.

Good morning, boys and girls. I need a volunteer this morning, someone who is really something special. This person must
love jelly beans. Is there anyone here who really likes jelly
beans? [*Let them answer, and pick a child who will partici-
pate in an enthusiastic way.*] Do you think that you really like
jelly beans? [*Let the child answer.*] I know that you cannot
eat all of the jelly beans that I have brought with me, so I am
going to give them to you, and you can save them in any way
that you want. [*Begin handing the child the jelly beans, and,
after he has eaten a few, you might suggest that he fill his pockets, take some back to his parents, fill his hands, or try anything so that he can take all of the jelly beans he can carry.*]
Now that you have all the jelly beans that you can carry, what
should I do with the ones that I have left? [*Let the child answer.*] Should I just throw them away, or wait until you come
back next week, or what should I do? [*Let him answer.*]

Did I ever tell you the story about the man in the Bible
who had such a wonderful year growing his crops that he filled
up all of his barns and still had things left over, so the only
thing he thought he could do was build some bigger barns?
Did I ever tell you this story? He didn't know what else to
do but to keep it all for himself. He never thought of sharing
it with the people who were hungry. He thought that God just
gave it all to him, and that God did not care if all of the rest
of the people went hungry or not. Our own friend did not think
of the rest of you either. He was like the rich farmer. Our own
friend kept all of the jelly beans to himself, just like the rest
of you may have done. When his pockets and hands, and even
his mouth were filled, he still wanted more if he could find
another place to put them. The rich farmer tore down his barns
that were filled and built bigger barns.

Jesus taught us something different. He said that God gives us all that we need, and it would be more than enough if we would share it with others.

Our friend could have shared his jelly beans with each of you, and would probably like to do so now. While he is sharing with you and feeling good about it, I hope that you will remember that you cannot take what God gives to your death, and that it is better if you share when you can.

What Is Your Treasure?

Luke 12:32-40, v. 34

For where your treasure is, there will your heart be also.

Objects: A pocket knife, a baseball glove, and a doll.

Good morning, boys and girls. How many of you have a treasure? [*Let them answer.*] Very good, a lot of you have some treasure. What kind of treasure do you have? [*Let them answer.*] I brought along some things that I thought might be a treasure to you. A treasure is something very important to you, something that is worth almost more than anything you can think of, when you think of things that you want or have.

When I was a boy, I always thought that my baseball glove was the most important treasure that I had, and I would not have given it up for anything. My brother always wanted a pocket knife that he could carry with him. When he was old enough to have a knife he got one, and he still carries it with him today. My sister was not too interested in ball gloves and pocket knives, but she loved her doll. That was really "it" for her, and she would take the doll with her wherever she went, even to bed when she went to sleep at night. She loved that doll with all of her heart, just like we loved our ball glove and knife.

Jesus knew how people love things, and he thought that this was all right, even good, as long as we remember what love is really meant to be. Jesus told us that we should not love gloves, knives, money, dolls, gold, cars, or anything more than we love people, and especially God. Loving our treasure can be wrong if we love it more than we love God and people. When we love our things more than we love God and people, it makes us greedy and unkind. Nothing is as important as God, and we should love him the most. Next to God is our love for each other, and when we share our love with each other instead of loving things, then we are also doing right. But if we love money or whatever is special to us, we end up trying to hurt others so that we can have more things. If we try to keep things such as food and clothes to ourselves, even when others need them, then we have wars or fights. But when you love God, it means that you will want to share the things that you have. You may even share your most important treasure, even if it is your ball glove or your knife or your doll. When you learn to share your treasure at your age, you will then be ready to share your money, your food, and whatever else is important to you when you grow older.

A Big Problem

Luke 12:49-53, v. 51

*Do you think that I have come to give peace on earth? No,
I tell you, but rather division.*

Objects: A blackboard, some chalk, and a division problem.

Good morning, boys and girls. Today we are going to get
back to school a little early. I want to work a math problem
on this board, so that I can teach you something about the
way God feels about the people of this world. All of us have
wondered why everyone does not believe and trust in God. Why
do certain people seem to do all of the things that God says
are wrong when God tells us that he loves all of us?

That is a big problem, but an old problem. I have a big
problem, too, and I want to figure it out, so I have brought
along my blackboard, my chalk, and my problem. This is my
problem. I can clean about four rooms in an hour at the
church. It must be done by tomorrow. The church is a big
place, and I think there are about thirty-two rooms in the whole
church. Some of the rooms are much bigger than others, but
some are also much smaller. I want to know how many people it will take to clean the church. Can you figure that problem
out for me? [*Let them answer, but go over the problem again.*]

The way to find the answer is to divide the number of rooms
that must be cleaned by the number of rooms that I can clean
in an hour. [*Do the problem.*] That means that I need eight
people if I want to do it in one hour, or four people if I want
to do it in two hours. To find the answer I must divide.

Jesus talked about dividing also. Some people thought that
Jesus just came to earth to bring us all together, and that it
did not make any difference what was right or wrong. They
thought Jesus was supposed to be like glue. But Jesus said that
this wasn't true. Some things are more important than this,

and so Jesus said he would be dividing us. There would be some people who would follow what he taught, and some people who would not follow what he taught. That means that they will be divided. It is the answer to the problem. Jesus is the divider. He teaches us right from wrong. He teaches us what is true and what is untrue. He tells us that we must follow him. If we do follow him, we are on one side. If we do not follow him, we are on the other side. Of course, the church is teaching us that we should do what Jesus teaches and follow him, but we all know that there is another side, and Jesus is not going to change to make the people who do wrong and believe wrong a part of his side.

Maybe the next time you are working a big problem that has to do with dividing, you will remember that Jesus is the big divider, and that we must choose which side we are going to be on.

Bearing Fruit for God

Luke 13:1-9, v. 9

"And if it bears fruit next year, well and good; but if not, you can cut it down."

Object: *Some fertilizer.*

Good morning, boys and girls. How many of you have ever tried to grow a plant or a tree? [*Let them answer.*] Did it live? [*Let them answer.*] How did you take care of your plant? [*Let them answer.*]

There is a story Jesus tells in the Bible about a man who had a fig tree planted on his farm. He asked another man who worked for him to take care of the tree. After a while, he came back to pick some of the fruit that had grown on the tree, but he was surprised to find that the tree had no figs. The owner was disappointed, and he told his worker to cut it down. But the worker asked him to give the tree one more chance. So the owner told him to give the tree some fertilizer, and that if it did not grow in one year, then he should cut it down.

Fertilizer helps plants to grow strong so that they will produce fruit, flowers, or whatever they are supposed to produce. If you want a strong plant, one that grows and grows, you must fertilize it. Fertilizer is very important for plants and trees.

Jesus told this story so that we would learn something very important about ourselves, too. Sin makes us weak. We all sin. Every one of us is a sinner. Sin makes us very weak and keeps us from living the way that God wants us to live. When we are weak, we cannot even do the good things that we want to do.

There is only one way to make things better so that we can get over our weakness. We must tell God how sorry we are for our sin. This is called repentance, and it is as good for us as fertilizer is for a plant.

Tell God that you are sorry, and ask him to forgive you, and you will get rid of your sin. When you do not have the sin, then you can grow strong and be the way that God wanted you to be.

The next time you see someone feeding a plant some fertilizer to help it grow strong, I hope you will remember how telling God you are sorry for your sin will also help you to grow strong. Will you do that? Good. God bless you very much.

Charley Becomes Happy

Luke 13:22-30, v. 30

"And behold, some are last who will be first, and some are first who will be last."

Object: *A folding chair.*

Good morning, boys and girls. Today I have a story to tell you about one of my favorite friends. His name is Charley, and I want you to know that Charley is a really good friend. It hasn't always been easy for Charley, because, you see, Charley is a folding chair. [*Show them a folding chair.*] How many of you have ever sat on a chair like Charley? [*Let them answer.*] Aren't they great? You can take a friend like Charley almost anywhere and sit on him. I have had Charley in the yard, in different rooms of the house, and all over the church. Charley certainly is a good friend.

Now let me tell you why it hasn't always been easy for Charley. When people are through with Charley, they fold him up and put him away. Many times, I guess almost all of the time, Charley is on the bottom of the stack. All of the other folding chairs are on top of him, and you can imagine how that must feel. It isn't too bad if they stack the other chairs right, but when they are put down on him the wrong way, it really hurts. But the worst part of all is that Charley is always the last folding chair to be used.

I tried to tell Charley that this wasn't so bad, but he didn't agree. I told him that he would not wear out so fast, but Charley likes to be used and sat on, since that is the reason why he was made. Charley really felt bad. But then one day that all changed.

He was still at the bottom, and that meant that he was the last chair used, but he was put up at the far end of a big hall. He heard it was going to be a very big dinner, and he was glad that they had to use all of the chairs, because it meant that he would be used also. When Charley was finally set up, he noticed that he was all alone at a very beautiful table. He was glad to be used, but now he was all alone and that made him sad. But he wasn't sad for long. Because into the hall came the president of our country, and he was taken to the front where the beautiful table was set. Then after everyone had clapped their hands until they hurt, the president sat down on Charley, and Charley felt good all over. Here he was — the president's chair. What a wonderful day for Charley.

That is a good lesson for all of us who sometimes feel unnoticed and not very important. Jesus told us that his kingdom is going to be made up of the people who may not have been very important in this world, and who, most of the time, felt that they were the last. But Jesus said that the last will be first in his world, and the first in this world will be last. The most important thing is to be loving and to want to be used like Charley the folding chair. Then some day you will have the most important place in the world, a place called the Kingdom of God.

What's in a Name?

Luke 13:31-35, v. 35

"Behold, your house is forsaken. And I tell you, you will not see me until you say, 'Blessed be he who comes in the name of the Lord!' "

Object: Some soda crackers like "Krispy" and "Zesta."

Good morning, boys and girls. Today we are going to talk about Jesus and how he came to share his life with us. Jesus represented God on earth. The Bible says that Jesus came in the name of the Lord. I want to show you what that means.

How many of you like crackers? [*Let them answer.*] Do you like your crackers in soup, or with peanut butter on them? [*Let them answer.*] Sometimes I like to eat my crackers just plain with nothing on them. I just like the salty taste. But that is not the important part of these crackers today. I want these crackers to teach you something about Jesus.

There are a lot of people who make soda crackers, and everyone who makes crackers thinks that these crackers are the very best crackers in the world. I have two kinds of crackers with me today. [*Show them the crackers.*] This cracker is called a "Krispy" cracker and it comes in a beautiful box that looks like this. [*Show them the box.*] How many of you have ever eaten a "Krispy" cracker? [*Let them answer.*]

Now here is a second soda cracker. It is called a "Zesta" cracker, and it comes in a box like this. [*Show them the box.*] How many of you have ever eaten a "Zesta" cracker? [*Let them answer.*]

Each of the crackers comes with a name. One is called a "Zesta Cracker," and one is called a "Krispy Cracker." You could say that this cracker comes in the name of "Krispy," and this one comes in the name of "Zesta."

Jesus said that he came in the name of the Lord. Jesus came

because God sent Jesus to represent him on earth among all of the people. Jesus comes in the name of the Lord, like a soda cracker comes in the name of "Krispy" or "Zesta." Of course, representing God is a lot more important than representing a cracker company, but I hope that you understand the idea.

When you eat a certain cracker you think of "Zesta" or "Krispy." When you think of Jesus you should think of God our Father in heaven. Is that who you think of when you hear about Jesus? If you do, then you know what Jesus meant when he said that he came in the "name of the Lord." God Bless You.

The Humble Teddy

Luke 14:1, 7-14, v. 11

"For every one who exalts himself will be humbled, and he who humbles himself will be exalted."

Object: A tire jack.

Good morning, boys and girls. How many of you have ever been with your father or mother when they had a flat tire on their car? [*Let them answer.*] Did it seem like a good time to them? Did they enjoy changing the tire? [*Let them answer.*] It isn't much fun, is it? As a matter of fact, it is an awful experience, and I don't know anyone who likes to change a tire. But if you think that it is bad for your father or mother, wait until you must do it. As bad as it is, though, I want you to know that it helped me to come to know one of my very best friends. How many of you have met my friend Teddy Tire Jack? [*Let them answer.*] I am sure that you have a friend like my friend Teddy, but I want you to know that he isn't easy to get to know. As a matter of fact, Teddy has been with me ever since I bought my car, and I did not get to meet him until the other day when I had a flat tire while driving in the country.

There I was driving along and having a good time, when, all of a sudden, I heard this funny noise and the car started to run funny. I knew that I had a flat tire. It seemed awful at first, but then I went to the trunk of my car and got out the spare tire, and began to think of what a dirty job it would be. As I told you, I had not met my friend Teddy until that moment, and when I got him out he looked like a lot of hard work for me. But Teddy was a surprise. Imagine how he worked to lift that heavy car so I could take the flat tire off and put on a new tire. It was wonderful the way he raised that car and did almost all of the work for me. It wasn't so bad after all, and I owe it all to Teddy the Tire Jack.

Jesus says that there are a lot of people who are his followers just like Teddy. We call them humble people, and they work hard, though very few people notice them. Teddy rides around in my trunk and never says a word. He is almost unnoticed until I have something awful happen like a flat tire, and then he is ready to help, even to lift a heavy car. That is something I cannot do, and look how much bigger I am than Teddy is. He holds the car up and, when he is done, I put him back in the trunk. I would say that Teddy is very humble.

That is the way that we should be. We don't have to ride in the trunk of a car, but we should remember how great our God is when we think of ourselves, and that will make us humble also. When God wants you, he will use you, and he will make you great just like I used Teddy and made him great. It is a hard lesson to learn when we talk about being humble, but it is the way that every Christian should feel when he thinks of his Lord Jesus Christ and his loving God.

It Costs to Follow Jesus

Luke 14:25-33, v. 28

For which of you, desiring to build a tower, does not first sit down and count the cost, whether he has enough to complete it?

Object: A bank book.

Good morning, boys and girls. Do any of you ever go to the bank with your mother or father? [*Let them answer.*] What do they do at a bank? [*Let them answer.*] That's right, they put money in the bank and they take money out of the bank. The bank is a place where they save their money, or a place where they can borrow money. I brought along a bank book that tells me how much money I have saved at this bank. It tells me how much I can spend if I want to build a new house, or buy a house or a car, or anything else that I think that I need to use my money for. That is very important because you do not want to spend more money than you have in the bank.

This little book tells me exactly how much I can spend. Just think how awful it would be if you decided to build a house with the money that you had in the bank, and then you made the house so big that you could not pay for it. The house would never get finished. You might only have three walls, or a house with no windows or doors. You must plan what you are going to do, and spend the right amount of money on it, but not too much.

Jesus told us that the same kind of thing is true about being his disciple. He says that being his disciple is not free. It is going to cost you something, and you must decide if it is worth it. It will cost you time. You must worship Jesus, if you are going to be his disciple. You can't stay home and read the funny papers and still be in church at the same time; but being a disciple says that you must worship Jesus. You must share your things with others, too. You cannot be a disciple of Jesus and be selfish. Jesus makes you promise him that you will be ready to share what you have with others. And you must be forgiving. That means when someone does something wrong to you and it makes you angry, you cannot stay angry. You must be ready to forgive the person who hurt you, and show him how much you love him. These are some of the things that you must do if you want to be a disciple of Jesus and follow him. We call these things "counting the cost." It is like building a house. If you want to build a house, then you must have some money in the bank. If you want to be a follower of Jesus, you must have love and be ready to share it with all of the people of this world. Being a Christian isn't cheap. It is very expensive because you must spend yourself, and follow the teachings of Jesus.

The next time that you go to a bank and see your mother or father look at their bank book, I hope that you will think about what it is costing you to be a Christian, and that you will be glad that you have your life to spend for Jesus. God bless you.

Happiness Is Finding the Lost

Luke 15:1-10, v. 8

"Or what woman, having ten silver coins, if she loses one coin, does not light a lamp and sweep the house and seek diligently until she finds it?"

Object: A coin.

Good morning, boys and girls. How many of you have ever lost some money? [*Let them answer.*] Was it a lot of money? [*Let them answer.*] I think that people really are upset when they lose money, because it is usually money that was needed to spend for food, or clothes, or maybe a gift for somebody that they loved. Money is very important to all of us because we use it to buy the things that we need. Our fathers and mothers work very hard for their money and, if they lose it, they usually hunt for it. How many of you have ever hunted for money? [*Let them answer.*] Did you find it? [*Let them answer.*] If you found it, I want you to remember if it made you happy? I know the answer to that question, because I have lost money and then found it, and it made me very happy.

Jesus knows how important money can be to all of us, and he told a story about a woman who lost some money, to show us how important people are to God. He said that when a woman lost some money, she hunted all day and night until she found it, and then when she found it, she celebrated by inviting all of her friends in to her home.

Jesus said that this is the way that God feels about people who become lost from him. He is sad that he lost them, but when he finds them he has a great celebration. Jesus did not mean that he forgot where he put one of us. Jesus did not mean that he dropped one of us in another country and did not bring us back home. Jesus talks about people being lost when they forget to worship him, or decide that they want to be their own gods, or when they hate others instead of loving people the way they were taught. These are the lost people, and God is very sad when he loses people.

If you would decide to stop coming to Sunday church school and church, or if you started to live differently by cheating your friends and lying to your parents, then God would think that you were lost from him. That would make him very sad. But if you also remembered what God had taught you, and decided that you wanted to be forgiven, and you asked God to be with you, then you would know how happy it made him feel to find you again. That is the thing that makes God the happiest: finding his children and bringing them back home to live with him and Jesus.

The next time that you lose a coin or any amount of money, and you feel bad, remember how bad God feels when he loses a person; but then when you find your money you will also know how much God loves bringing back the people who were lost.

Call in the Clowns!

Luke 15:1-3, 11-32, v. 24

"For this my son was dead, and is alive again; he was lost, and is found." And they began to make merry.

Objects: Some horns, drums, and other party items.

Good morning, boys and girls. How many of you like a good party? [*Let them answer.*] Do you remember the last party that you went to? [*Let them answer.*] I brought along some things that I thought might help us think about a party. [*Pass out the party toys.*] If we were planning a really special party, we might even call in some clowns. Wouldn't that be an exciting way to have a party?

When do we have parties? [*Let them answer.*] That's right, birthdays and other times when we want to celebrate something that is really happy or important.

Jesus told a story about a father who had two sons. The older son was always good to his father and worked hard on their farm. But the younger son did not like to work and asked for his share of the family's money, then ran away to have a good time. It wasn't too long until he had spent all of the money, and he was broke. He got a job taking care of some pigs, but he also had to live with the pigs. Finally, one day, he made up his mind to go back and ask his father to forgive him. So he went back, but before he could say anything to his father about how sorry he was, his father ran out to greet him and tell him how much he had missed him. Finally, the father had a big party to celebrate his son's happy return.

Jesus told this story to show us how glad God is when we change our minds, and come back to tell him how sorry we are for our sins. God is so happy to have us back that it is almost like a party in heaven.

God loves us a lot, and he misses us when we leave him

to go off in another direction. But God is so happy when we come back, that it is like a very happy and wonderful party.

It isn't easy to come back to God. Sometimes we are afraid, or we think that God doesn't want us when we have been bad, but this isn't true. God always loves us and is really pleased when we change our minds and come back to him.

Remember, going back to God is like being a part of a party in heaven. We don't know whether there will be any clowns, but we do know we will have a wonderful time there!

A Candle with Two Wicks

Luke 16:1-13, v. 13

"No servant can serve two masters; for either he will hate the one and love the other or he will be devoted to the one and despise the other. You cannot serve God and mammon."

Object: A candle with the wick exposed at both ends.

Good morning, boys and girls. Today we are going to try something that we have heard about, but have seldom seen. I brought a candle along with me that is a very special candle. I want to show it to you. [*Show them the candle.*] What is different about this candle? [*Let them answer.*] That's right, there is a wick on each end. Have you ever heard about burning the candle at both ends? Older people talk about burning the candle at both ends when they are doing too many things and not getting enough rest. But I want to show it to you today for another reason. Suppose your electricity went out at home and you wanted or needed some light. You could light this end of the candle as I am doing now and it would give you light. Do you like candlelight? [*Let them answer.*] That's nice, but it isn't bright enough for me, so I have this special candle, and I think I will light the other end as well. Now I have twice as much light from the same candle. How do you like the candlelight now? [*Let them answer.*] But all of a sudden I have a terrible problem. First of all I cannot set the candle down, and second, it is dripping all over me. I mean this is terrible. Now I don't know which end to put out. It gets so confusing. I know that it is the same candle, but this end seems brighter then the other end. But the other end seems to burn more evenly. What should I do? I just hate to make decisions like this. As a matter of fact, I am beginning to hate one end of this candle. I just don't know which end I hate and which end I love. It is confusing.

The same thing is true of you and me that is true of the candle. We were made by God, to serve and love God. But the devil seems like so much more fun sometimes that we think maybe we should be on the devil's side. Of course we can't be on both sides. That is when everything seems so confusing.

Jesus tells us that we must choose one side or the other. There is no way that we can serve both God and someone else. It is Jesus' advice of course, that we make up our minds to serve God and to forget the other side. If we don't, Jesus says, we will end up hating one and loving the other, or hating the other and loving the one. Each of us must decide who we are going to love. I am going to love God, and I hope that he is your choice also. Remember what happened to the person who burned the candle at both ends, and then choose who you are going to serve.

Warning!

Luke 16:19-31, vv. 27-28

"And he said, 'Then I beg you, father, to send him to my father's house, for I have five brothers, so that he may warn them, lest they also come into this place of torment.' "

Object: A warning device, like a siren or buzzer.

[*Begin with your warning device.*] What was that, boys and girls? How many of you have heard something like that before? [*Let them answer.*] Do you know why we use a siren? [*Let them answer.*] That's right, we want to warn people to get out of the way, to tell them someone is coming who needs to get somewhere in a hurry, and that they want everyone else to get out of the way until they get there. Ambulances use them, fire departments use them, and sometimes the police use them. A siren is a very important thing, and it keeps us from having big wrecks and hurting other people. Of course, you must listen to the warning and pull over if you are driving. A warning is not any good if you don't pay attention to it. Some children do not pay attention to the warnings that their fathers and mothers give them, and they get hurt. I know a child who was warned not to play with matches, and he did. Do you know what happened? [*Let them fill in the answer.*] That's right, he was burned.

Jesus tells us about the warnings that we have gotten in the Bible from God about the way that we should behave, and what will happen to us if we do not listen to the teachings. He said that the reason these things were written was not to scare us, but to warn us so that something terrible would not happen to us. I think that this is a very loving thing for God to do. He warns us about the bad things so that they will not hurt us and cause us great harm.

Jesus told stories like this to the disciples and to everyone else who wanted to listen. Some people listened and did what he told them not to do anyway. Those people did not listen to the warning. They suffered what they thought was an awful accident. But it was not an accident, because they had been warned. If you hear a siren and still try to drive down the middle of the street where the fire engine or ambulance is coming, you will have a terrible accident and cause other people to get hurt as well. The same thing is true about not listening to God's warnings that he gives us in the Bible. If we hear the warnings and still cause the trouble, then it is not an accident. We will be hurt, and others will be hurt also because we did not listen. When you read the Ten Commandments, and they warn you about how to live, then you should pay attention to them the same way that you do to a siren. They are God's warning to teach us how to live safely.

Homework Is a Duty

Luke 17:1-10, v. 10

"So you also, when you have done all that is commanded you, say, 'We are unworthy servants; we have only done what was our duty.' "

Objects: *Some homework papers.*

Good morning, boys and girls. How many of you are glad to be in school? [*Let them raise their hands.*] Most of you like to go to school, but some of you are not too happy about it. Not all of us like the same things, but I am glad that most of you like to go to school. School is really very important, because it is there where we learn to read and write and work with numbers. All of those things and many others are really very important, and school is the place where we learn them. How many of you have homework to bring home with you after school is out? [*Let them answer.*] Do you like to do homework? Most boys and girls like to play outside, or watch TV, or do something else when they come home instead of doing their homework. But still we must do it. It is our duty. How many of you know what the word "duty" means? [*Let them answer.*] Most all of you know the word "duty." It is when we have something to do that is our responsibility, something that we do not receive special thanks for doing. It is something that is expected.

I think that there are things like that between us and God. There are some things that are our duty to God, and we should not expect God to send us a special message of thanks, or have one of his workers pat us on the back, for doing it.

I know some people who think that they are doing God a favor when they come to church or Sunday church school. That is not a favor, or something that you should be thanked for doing. That is your duty. Some people think that they should be thanked for telling the truth or helping someone who needs help. If you see someone who needs you, then you should help them because you are a Christian. We don't need to be thanked and patted on the back for doing good things, because that is what we are supposed to do.

No one thanks you for doing your homework. Doing homework is your duty. No one should thank you for doing Christian things, either, because you also have Christian things to do. That's what Jesus thought, and he told the disciples that very thing one day when they asked him about doing special things to be special people. Do what is right, and you will be doing your Christian duty. The next time that you do some homework and you think about it, I hope that you think about your Christian duties, and then remember to do them.

Ten Broken Pencils

Luke 17:11-19, vv. 17-18

Then said Jesus, "Were not ten cleansed? Where are the nine? Was no one found to return and give praise to God except this foreigner?"

Objects: *Ten pencils with broken points and one pencil sharpener.*

Good morning, boys and girls. How many of you like to write with pencils? [*Let them answer.*] Good pencils are very hard to find. Whenever I am looking for a pencil, I either cannot find one, or when I find the pencil, it has a broken point, or has never been sharpened. Do you have that problem? [*Let them answer.*] I have a little story to tell you about ten pencils that I found around my house, and every one of them was either broken or had never been sharpened. This is their story.

I found these pencils in different places. One of them was on my dresser, several of them were in a kitchen drawer where they had been for several years. I even found one of them on the kitchen floor beneath the refrigerator. It seemed like everywhere I went I found a pencil, but all of them were broken in one way or another. On a shelf in a beautiful tea cup, I found some paper clips, rubber bands, and another pencil. Of course it was broken also. There were others in different places, like on top of the washer, since someone had forgotten to empty his pockets before sending his slacks to the laundry. There was another on my workbench, one in the garage, and a couple behind the cushions of the couch. Every one of them was broken, and they looked sad in their terrible condition.

A pencil is meant to have a sharp point and to write; to leave them in this kind of condition was awful. So I decided to do what I thought should be done. I got out my special pencil sharpener and went right to work. Soon each pencil I sharpened looked happy and relieved to be back at work again.

I could hardly work fast enough, I felt so good. But as I finished sharpening one and putting it down, it would disappear before I could pick up another. All ten pencils were sharpened like they had never been sharpened before, and not one of them who left even said thank you. Excuse me, that isn't true. There was one that said thank you. The one that I found on the floor under the refrigerator. It came back to tell me how grateful it was for what I had done for it.

You know the story of my pencils is not original. Jesus told a similar story about something even more important. He told about healing ten men, only one of whom thanked God for what happened. I hope that you remember the story, but I hope even more that you remember to thank God every day for the wonderful things that he does for you. That is one of the most important parts of our life — to be grateful to God, and to praise him for all of the glorious things that he does to help us.

Jesus Is a Ladder to Us

Luke 19:1-10, v. 9

And Jesus said to him, "Today salvation has come to this house, since he also is a son of Abraham."

Object: A ladder.

Good morning, boys and girls. Today we are going to talk about rescuing someone whom we love very much. Let's pretend that there is someone caught in a house that is burning and she cannot get out by the door, but she is too high to jump without really getting hurt. What will we do to rescue this person? [*Let them answer.*] Those are good answers. We could do a lot of those things, but maybe the best answer is to put our ladder up against the house and either climb up the ladder and help her out, or let her just climb down the ladder. Either way we have helped to rescue her.

Let's pretend again. Suppose that someone has fallen through the ice while he was ice skating. You want to help him but the ice is too thin to walk on, so what can you do? [*Let them answer.*] That's right, you can put the ladder down on the ice and let the person grab hold of it and pull himself to the shore. Sometimes you can even crawl out on a ladder to rescue someone in the water when you can't walk on the ice.

Those are just two ways that you can save someone or rescue them with your ladder.

Jesus is like a ladder to us. Jesus rescued us, or saved us, from death when he died on the cross. That was the biggest saving job that anyone ever did. When Jesus came to earth to save you and me from our sins, we never knew what a great job he did until after he died on the cross. We knew that we had committed a few sins here and there, and that we were not the kind of people that God wanted us to be. But we were not sure that we were as bad as we were until we knew how perfect Jesus was. Jesus did not have any sin, and still he loved us so much that he died for us so that we could live with God forever. That is a great love, and a real rescue job. Jesus saved us from our sins and made us good enough to live with God forever.

The next time that you see a ladder or hear about someone rescuing someone else with a ladder, perhaps you will think about today and how Jesus is like a ladder. He comes to us, stretches out, and saves us from whatever our sins are. Jesus is a great Savior, which means that he rescues us from our sin.

The Shouting Stones
[Appropriate for use on Palm Sunday]
Luke 19:28-40, v.40

He answered, "I tell you, if these wer silent, the very stones would cry out."

Objects: *Some small stones. Have enough so that each child may receive one.*

Good morning, boys and girls. Today is Palm Sunday and it is one of the very biggest days in our church year. Can you imagine how excited you would have been if you had been one of Jesus' disciples and walked beside him, while he rode a small donkey into the great city of Jerusalem? The crowds were cheering, and waving their palm branches, and throwing their coats on the road, so that the road looked like it had been carpeted. You would have loved it.

Of course not everyone was happy about Jesus coming into Jerusalem. There were some of the people who called themselves the leaders of the Jews, who thought Jesus was dangerous and working against them. They wanted Jesus to go away and be silent. If Jesus would become king like the people wanted, then they knew that they could no longer be the leaders.

But the people kept shouting and waving their banners. Everywhere you went you could hear things being said like "Blessed is the King who comes in the name of the Lord." Those were dangerous words, and frightening words, to the people who disliked Jesus. These men told Jesus to tell his disciples to be quiet. But they would not be quiet. The disciples had waited a long time for a day like this and they loved it. Other people who had only heard of Jesus began to shout and sing the same things that the disciples were shouting. Now the leaders were really angry, and they commanded Jesus to quiet the disciples. But Jesus was not afraid of these men, and he knew that this day belonged to God. He looked at the men who were angry with him, and told them that even if they could make his disciples silent, the stones on the ground would begin singing and shouting the same things that the disciples were singing and shouting. Stones just like these stones were all over the road, and they would have made a mighty sound if they could have spoken. The leaders knew that there was nothing they could do that day. It was the day for Jesus and for the people who believed in him.

I want you to have one of these stones, so that you will remember Palm Sunday as the day that Jesus rode into Jerusalem and his disciples made a great chorus, proclaiming Jesus as "the King who came in the name of the Lord." It will also help you to remember that even if not one human voice said that Jesus was the Christ, God would make sure that we still would know it — even if he had to make the stones shout that Christ was the King.

More Important Than We Thought

Luke 20:9-19, v. 17

But he looked at them and said, "What then is this that is written: 'The very stone which the builders rejected has become the head of the corner'?"

Object: A garage sale item, such as a lamp or a picture.

Good morning, boys and girls. How many of you have ever been to a garage sale? [*Let them answer.*] Did you have fun? [*Let them answer.*] Did you buy anything? [*Let them answer.*]

[*Hold up picture.*] A couple months ago I bought a picture at a garage sale. It is a nice picture, but nothing really special. Someone wanted to get rid of it and did not think it was very special either. After I bought it, took it home, and cleaned it up, I found that it was really very special. A lot of people would really like to have this picture, because it is painted by a very famous artist and is quite valuable. Here I have something that no one thought was important, and now I find it is very important.

That is the way that it is with Jesus. When Jesus was alive and teaching, there were some people who thought that he was just another man and nothing special. There were other people who thought that they could get rid of Jesus and no one would ever miss him. As a matter of fact, there were some people who wanted to get rid of Jesus and were even willing to murder him if they could. They really hated him.

But after Jesus did die on the cross, the people found out how important he really was to this world. Jesus was the most important person who ever lived, but most people did not know it until after he had died.

Jesus is like a picture that no one knows is important until after it is gone, or sold to someone else. Jesus became so important to us because, when he died, he saved us all from our sins.

Some people wanted to get rid of him, and they never knew how important he was until after he died. Then they knew that Jesus was the most important person who ever lived.

A Different Kind of King

Luke 23:35-43, vv. 36-37

The soldiers also mocked him, coming up and offering him vinegar, and saying, "If you are the King of the Jews, save yourself."

Object: A cup of vinegar.

Good morning, boys and girls. We refer to Jesus as the King, and he was a kind of king different from the king of a country. Jesus was King over all the earth. People did not always know what kind of king he was. Some people thought that he would make a good king of the land in which he lived. They tried to make him a king who lived in a palace, made laws, and collected taxes. But Jesus was not that kind of a king.

The people who were kings and were close to kings were afraid of Jesus because they thought he wanted their jobs, or would give their jobs to his friends. They did not know that Jesus was sent by God to start a new kind of world over which he would be king. Jesus is the King of Peace and Love on earth, and of the new world where all of the people who believe in him will live after they die. That is the kind of king that Jesus is now and was then. But the people did not know it.

You have heard how they hung him on a cross and killed him. While he was hanging on the cross, they thought that he could not hurt them, and, though they were a little bit afraid of him, they teased him terribly. One of the things they did was make fun of his being a king. They gave him a crown that was made out of thorns. That was awful and it hurt when they shoved it down on his head. One of the other things they did was to give him something to drink. I have something like what they gave him that day, and I thought that you might want to smell it. [*Give them the cup to pass around and ask them what they think it is.*] That's right, it is vinegar. Can you imagine drinking vinegar? [*Let them answer.*] Jesus was thristy, but they thought in their own evil way that they were having fun with a dying man whom many called their king. It was awful at that moment.

But things got better. Jesus died and you know he was buried, and many thought that this was the last they would ever hear about him. But he fooled them by coming back to life and starting the kingdom that he always promised would happen. We are part of Jesus' world, and citizens of his kingdom. We are so happy that Jesus is not a king like other kings, but instead, is a king forever. This was God's plan, and it is the best plan for a king that anyone ever had.

Gum!

[Appropriate for use at Easter]

Luke 24:1-11, v. 3

But when they went in they did not find the body.

Objects: *Some packs of gum with the sticks of gum removed and the wrappers replaced in the packages.*

Good morning, boys and girls. How many of you know what today is and what it means? [*Let them answer.*] That's right, it is Easter, but what is Easter all about? [*Let them answer.*] Right, today is the day that we celebrate to remember when God raised Jesus from the dead. We all remember how awful it was when Jesus was crucified on the cross, and we were sorry that he died. But now we know that God did not forget him. Instead, he made him come back from the dead. What a wonderful day Easter is for all of us.

Do you remember the story of how the women who were friends of Jesus came up to where he was buried, and how they met an angel who talked to them? Do you remember how surprised they were to find out something that they did not expect? I have something with me this morning to help you remember how the women felt when they came to the tomb. I know all of you like what I brought, and I am going to share it with you. [*Begin to pass out the empty wrappers of gum.*] How many of you know what this is? [*Let them answer.*] Gum. Do you like gum? [*Let them answer.*] Well, I am going to let you chew your piece of gum if you want to, as soon as you get it unwrapped. [*As they discover that there is not any gum inside the wrapper, share their amazement with them.*] Isn't that a shock! When you get a piece of paper wrapped like that, you expect that there will be a piece of gum inside it, don't you? [*Let them answer.*] That is the way it is supposed to be.

That is also the way that the women felt when they arrived

at the place where Jesus was buried and found that Jesus was not there. He had died, they saw him die. He was buried in the tomb. They had seen him being taken to the tomb. When dead people are put in tombs, they stay in tombs. But Jesus was not there, and the women were surprised. Now an angel of God met them in the place where Jesus had been buried and told them that Jesus was living, and that he was no longer in the tomb. What a wonderful surprise. Jesus was dead, but now he is alive. I have a surprise for you also. [*Bring out a plate with the missing sticks of gum.*] Here are the sticks of gum that you thought were buried in the paper wrappers. As you can see, they are alive and well. This is just a reminder for you, so that you will never forget that while Jesus was not in the tomb, he was alive and well, and still lives today as the Christ, the Son of the Living God.

You Can't Hide the Light

John 1:1-18, v. 5

The light shines in the darkness, and the darkness has not overcome it.

Object: A box with a hole in one end and a blanket that will shut out the light attached to the other end.

Good morning, boys and girls. Today we are going to have a little fun and also learn something about Jesus. I brought a special box with me that I want to share with you. I want you to put your head in the box and shut out all of the light with the blanket. I want you to see how dark it is inside of that box. Then when you tell me that it is dark, really dark, I am going to open up this tiny hole in the other end of the box and see if you can see the light, and also if the light lets you see the inside of the box.

[*Begin the experiment with several of the children.*] The whole box is dark. We have a lot of darkness and only one small bit of light. What I want you to learn is that all of the darkness in the whole world cannot shut out a little bit of light. The little bit of light can be seen in the biggest amount of darkness. Do you understand what I mean?

The reason that we shared this little experiment is because it is what the Bible teaches us about Jesus. Jesus is like the light. He is only one person in the world, but he is such a strong person that he can overcome, or be stronger than, all of the rest of the people in the world. Jesus is light, Jesus is good. There is nothing wrong with Jesus at all, and wherever Jesus is, he will bring his goodness with him. Let's say that there is a lot of sin in the world. All of us make sin, and are a part of sin. There is so much sin in the world you might think that we could not get rid of it. But that is not true. Jesus is like the light in the darkness. He gets rid of the sin by just being there. When you have sin in your heart, and you can have a lot of it, then ask Jesus to share your life with you, and your sin will go away. Jesus will forgive you your sin and you will have no more.

That is why I want you to put your head in the box. The box is like a world full of sin. We don't think that we will ever get rid of sin, but the Bible teaches us that when Jesus came into the world, he was like a light, and wherever he went he made the darkness, or the sin, leave so that people could live without living in sin.

Maybe you want to make your own box when you go home. Then you can remember how glad we are to have Jesus in our lives so that we don't live in the dark, but rather in the light. God bless you all.

Now What Do We Do?

John 2:1-11, vv. 9-10

When the steward of the feast tasted the water now become wine, and did not know where it came from (though the servants who had drawn the water knew), the steward of the feast called the bridegroom and said to him, "Every man serves the good wine first; and when men have drunk freely, then the poor wine; but you have kept the good wine until now."

Objects: Some wine and some water.

Good morning, boys and girls. I want to tell you a story this morning, and I hope it will help you to believe something wonderful about the person we know as Jesus.

Jesus was invited to a wedding in a town called Cana. The people to be married were either close friends of Jesus, or of his family, because we know that his mother was at the wedding, too. Jesus came to the wedding with his disciples and met his mother there. The disciples were fairly new, since Jesus had just begun his ministry a short time before. They had not been at the wedding very long when the people who were in charge ran out of refreshments. No doubt some of the people had been there a lot longer than Jesus and the disciples, so they did as people do today. They ate and drank almost everything that was given to them.

What do you do when you run out of refreshments at your parties? [*Let them answer.*] That's right, you get some more refreshments. The only problem was that the people at the wedding were drinking some very good wine and there was no place to get more. Mary knew that her son was someone very special, and that he could take care of almost any problem. She also knew that Jesus was not a magician. He did not trick people, or switch things so fast with his hands that people could not see what was happening. Jesus solved problems in only one way, and that was through his Father in heaven. Mary did not know what Jesus would do, but she was certain he could do something if it was wanted by God.

It takes a long time to make wine. There are good wines, and bad wines. Jesus told the people who were working at the party to take some very large jars and fill them with water. They did as they were told and then brought the jars back to the party. [*Show the children the water.*] When the people went over to the jars and filled their glasses, they filled them with wine. [*Show the wine.*] No one knew what had happened, except Mary, the people working at the party, and the disciples of Jesus. But I want you to know that, from that time on, those people knew that Jesus was someone very special with a power that no one else had. Do you think that you could change this water [*hold up the water*] to this wine? [*Hold up the wine.*] That's right, you could not. Maybe the next time you hear of someone running out of something to eat or drink, you will remember the day that Jesus took some clear water and turned it into the best wine that anyone had ever drunk.

Combination Locks and Freedom

John 8:31-36, v. 32

"And you will know the truth, and the truth will make you free."

Object: A combination lock.

Good morning, boys and girls. Does anyone have a combination lock? [*Let them answer.*] If you have a combination lock, that is, a lock that has a lot of numbers on it, tell me what you use it for? [*Let them answer.*] A lot of boys and girls have a combination lock to use on their bicycles. They ride their bikes to school or to the park, and while they are in school or playing, they know that their bikes are safely locked. Once you lock your bike up with a lock like this, then it cannot be moved or taken. Of course, you must remember the combination so that you can open the lock after you have used it. That means that you must have the right numbers and know how to turn the lock in the right directions so that it will open. Knowing the combination is very important, and it is the only thing that can make something locked be free again.

I think that a combination is like the truth. Combinations open locks or free things that are locked up. The truth makes things free also, according to Jesus. When we know the truth about anything, we work with it and get the right answers to whatever problem we have. For instance, when we know the truth about Jesus and that he is the Savior of the world, then we know a truth that is very important.

It means that we can stop worrying about a lot of things. We can stop worrying about dying. How many of you ever have worried about dying? [*Let them answer.*] That is a big worry to a lot of people who do not know that Jesus promises us a much longer life in his new world than in this world. Once you know the truth, then you are free from worry. The truth is that Jesus forgives sins. If you are worried about your sins, like the time that you told a lie to your mother or brother, and you ask Jesus to forgive you for the sin, and he does, then you can quit worrying about the sin.

The truth makes you free. You do not have to worry or fuss about something when you know the truth. Jesus says that he is the truth. There is nothing about Jesus that is a lie. Whatever he does or says is the truth.

That is why I like to think about the truth as being the combination. It is the right combination, and it makes us just as free as if we have a bicycle lock with a combination and we spin it to the right numbers. If we do it right, then the bicycle lock will come free just as you and I do when we follow Jesus. Jesus is the truth, and Jesus makes us free.

Do You Know His Voice?

John 10:22-30, v. 27

"My sheep hear my voice, and I know them, and they follow me."

Objects: *Some blindfolds.*

Good morning, boys and girls. How many of you think that you know the voices of other people? I wonder if you would know your mother's voice or your father's voice, or even my voice if you could not see me. Would you like to try? [*Let them answer.*] I have some blindfolds that I want you to put on and wear for a few minutes. While I am helping you put on your blindfolds, I want to invite some of your parents to come up front with us. We are going to let them talk to one another while you are blindfolded, and when you hear your mother or father speak, and you are sure that it is your parent talking then, you should walk toward them and hold out your hand. We will see if you know their voices as well as you think you do.

[*Help them put on their blindfolds. Invite the parents to gather around and begin to talk about anything. You can suggest that they talk about what they did this morning before they came to church. It might help if you took each child by the hand and walked him close to the parents. When they have all found their children, or their children have found them, you can invite them to remain for the rest of the sermon.*] That was a lot of fun, and we really learned something. Most of us really do know the voices of our parents, don't we? We did this experiment for a very good reason which I am going to share with you right now.

Jesus liked to talk about himself as being a shepherd. He thought that this was a good way to explain how God and people worked together. God is the shepherd, and we are like the sheep. A shepherd takes very good care of his sheep, but the sheep are allowed to do a lot of things on their own. A good shepherd is so close to his sheep that the sheep recognize the shepherd's voice. If there were a lot of sheep and a lot of shepherds together, the sheep would always know the voice of their shepherd, and gather around him.

That is the way it is with Christians. Jesus is our shepherd and we belong to him. When Jesus speaks, we should hear his voice and do what he tells us to do. We should also follow him and behave ourselves in the way that we know that Jesus would behave himself. The voices of the people whom we love are very important to us, and we like to hear them because they make us feel safe and loved. Jesus has a voice like that, and, though we cannot hear it in the same way, we are sure that he speaks to us in our prayers and through the Bible. Of course, that means that we must pray and listen to the Bible; and when we do, we know that Jesus will be just like a shepherd. The next time that you hear the voice of someone whom you cannot see, I want you to think about today and remember that Jesus speaks to us in many ways to show us how much he loves and cares for us.

A Light Bulb and God

John 13:31-35, v. 31

When he had gone out, Jesus said, "Now is the Son of man glorified, and in him God is glorified."

Objects: A light bulb inside of a light globe.

Good morning, boys and girls. Today we are going to talk about the way Jesus, and the person whom we call God, are the same. Sometimes this is a very hard thing to explain, but I hope I can make it somewhat easier with the object that I have brought with me this morning. How many of you think that Jesus was part of God's plan? [*Let them answer.*] Very good, Jesus was part of God's plan. But Jesus was more than just another man who loved God and did what God wanted him to do. God was in Jesus in a very special way, so special that we must say that God and Jesus are one person. Now let me show you what I mean. I brought a light bulb with me, and I am going to call the light bulb "God." As you can see, the light bulb is a very bright light, and it shines in a very special way. Wherever this light shines, the darkness goes away. I also have a globe that fits over the light bulb, so that when the light shines you cannot see it shine, but you can see the light through the globe. I am going to call the globe "Jesus." Let's put the light inside of the globe and turn it on, so that you can share with me the idea that when the bulb is turned on, both the bulb and the globe are shining.

Now I told you that Jesus and God are one, and that is true. When we talk about one, we are talking about the other; and when we talk about the other, we are talking about one. It is the same with the light. When I tell you to turn on the light, I do not tell you to turn on the light bulb so that the globe will give us light. I just tell you to turn on the light, and I know that we are talking about the bulb and the globe.

Jesus warned us to know how close he and God were to one another. He said that when we talked about one, we talked about the other. He also said that when one of them did something wonderful, the other one shared in the wonderful thing that happened because they were one. God came to us in the form of Jesus, but when Jesus went back to God, they were the same again. I know that this is a very hard thing to understand, but I also hope that the next time you see a light, it will help you to remember that there is only one light, even though there is one bulb and one globe on the ceiling or on the wall. Just remember that Jesus and God are one, and that we worship our Jesus as our God. Will you do that? Good. God bless you very much.

Do You Believe What He Said?

John 14:23-29, v. 29

*"And now I have told you before it takes place, so that when
it does take place, you may believe."*

Objects: *Some nut cups, some wet cotton for each cup, and a package of
dry lima beans.*

Good morning, boys and girls. We are going to do something exciting today, but we will not know what a great day
it is until a week or so from now. How many of you have ever
heard the saying that "seeing is believing"? That means that
it is very hard to believe something unless you see it with your
own eyes. A lot of people feel like this, and they have a hard
time believing you, unless you can show them the proof.

People have always been like this, and they were this way
even with Jesus. It did not make any difference that Jesus
healed people and did all kinds of other miracles; they still
wanted the proof over and over again before they would believe him.

That was the reason that one day he told them how much
better life would be for them when he left them and sent the
Holy Spirit to take his place, while he went back to the Father
in heaven. People found that rather hard to believe, but he
told them anyway. He told them then, so that when the things
happened that he said were going to happen, they could remember that this was a promise of Jesus. Then they would think,
"Jesus told us it was going to happen and now we know that
he was right."

I have an experiment that I want to share with you this
morning that you are going to love. I have some beans with
me that I am going to give you to take home. By this time
next week they are going to be plants. That's the truth, and
to show you how fast they are going to grow, I am going to

have you grow them in this little nut cup with some cotton. Now you don't have to put them in water, plant them in the ground, or anything like you usually do. All I want you to do is to put them inside the wet cotton in the cup, and then come back and tell me next week if they did what I said they would do. Remember, I told you that they would grow into plants. I am doing this because I know that some of you will not believe me until it happens, but I know it will happen. This is the way that Jesus told the disciples and others about his great promises. They just had to wait until the things happened that he said were going to happen before they could find out if he was telling the truth. I can tell you now that whatever he promised was going to happen did happen. Jesus knew exactly what was going to take place, and it did.

I think that you will remember how much Jesus knew when you try our little experiment and watch your bean grow this week into a plant. When that bean becomes a plant, then I want you to remember the day that Jesus told everyone what was going to happen before it did, so that they would believe that Jesus was the Christ, the Son of the Living God. If you remember that, then you, too, will also believe that he was the Son of God.

It's Not on Any Map

John 15:26-27; 16:4b-11, v. 5

But now I am going to him who sent me; yet none of you asks me, "Where are you going?"

Object: A large map of the world, or any map of Israel.

Good morning, boys and girls. Today we are going to take a look at a large map that I brought with me, because I read something in the Bible that I thought we should answer. You will remember that some time ago we talked about how Jesus was crucified and buried, and how three days later he came back to life in what we call the resurrection. How many of you remember us talking about that time? [*Let them answer.*] After the resurrection, Jesus walked and talked with his disciples for almost seven weeks. One time he met some of them on a road while they were walking. Another time he met with them in a room in Jerusalem. Then, once, he actually cooked their breakfast on the shore of the lake and invited them to come and share not only the food, but also some talk with him. Jesus was very much alive after the resurrection. But this day he asked them a question and I think that it is a good one to ask you also. He said to them that he keeps telling them that he is going away, but that not one of them asked him, "Where are you going?" When you hear that Jesus is leaving, do you ever think about asking him where he is going?

I brought along a map today to ask you if you know where Jesus went when he left the disciples? [*Let them answer.*] Do you think you could find on the map the place where Jesus went after he left the disciples? [*Have some of them look at the map to see if they will point out a place.*] Do you think Jesus went to America or Egypt or Germany, or to any of the towns close by in Israel? [*Let them answer.*] Where do you think that Jesus went, and why is it important for us to know where he went when he left the disciples?

I will tell you why it is important. The reason that Jesus told the disciples that he was going away was because he wanted them to know where he was going. He did not want them to think that he was hiding, or just going to another town. He wanted them to know that the place he was going was the most special part of the whole plan of God. Now do you know where Jesus went when he left the disciples? [*Let them answer.*]

That's right, he went back to live with God in heaven, or the place that we call heaven. I don't mean the sky, but a real world where God is making a place for us to live after all of us die. Jesus is here on earth, but we cannot see him or touch him or feel him. Jesus is not in a body like ours any longer. But Jesus is alive and well and living with the Father. You can't find the place that he is staying on a map, but someday we will join him wherever he is, and we are going to love it more than anything we have ever loved. You can't find Jesus on a map, but you can be sure that Jesus knows where we are and what we are doing. Someday we will be with Jesus, and then we will be the happiest people that you ever knew. I can hardly wait. Can you? God bless you.

The Funnel of God

When the Spirit of truth comes, he will guide you into all the truth; for he will not speak on his own authority, but whatever he hears he will speak, and he will declare to you the things that are to come.

Object: A funnel.

Good morning, boys and girls. Have you ever tried to pour something from one bottle into another bottle? [*Let them answer.*] Do you usually spill some of it when you try to do this? [*Let them answer.*] Do you know how to keep from spilling whatever you have in the bottle? [*Let them answer.*] You can be extra careful, but I have a better way. How many of you have ever used a funnel? [*Let them answer.*] Tell me how you use one of these things that we call a funnel. [*Allow someone to give an explanation.*] That's right, you put the funnel into one of the bottles and then pour whatever you have into that bottle. The funnel acts like a guide, and it puts the thing that you are pouring in just the right place so nothing is spilled or lost. A funnel is a very helpful tool.

I would like us to think that the funnel is like the Spirit of God. We can try to do things on our own. We can look at the trees and the birds and bees, and see how God has made them, and the way that he takes care of them, and we can try to understand how God wants us to live. We can read books and talk to other people, but that does not really tell us how God loves us as people. We want to feel our love from God, and not find it out in any other way. The Bible tells us that the Spirit of God is like a funnel. The Spirit is a guide who brings the love of God right to us without spilling one drop. The Spirit does not change a word of what he hears when he speaks to us. He is really like a funnel. Whatever God wants us to know, the Spirit of God tells us. The Spirit of God works with us as children of God to help us learn every day something new about God and God's church. The Spirit teaches us how to forgive and how to be honest with each other. The Spirit does not make this up, but rather he brings it to us from God, without losing one part of what God wanted us to know. I suppose that this is why I tell you that the Spirit is like a funnel.

The next time that you see someone filling the gas tank on their mower with a funnel, or you see your father or mother using a funnel in the kitchen, I want you to think about all of the different ways that a funnel is used. Then I want you to think about the way that the Spirit of God is like a funnel, and the very many ways that the Spirit is used by God in teaching us. You must remember that the funnel does not make the stuff that it helps to pour. It comes from somewhere else. The same thing is true of the Spirit. The Spirit does not make up what he teaches us. The things that the Spirit pours into us are the good stuff that comes from God. The Spirit is like a funnel carrying the good news from God to us.

You Are Jesus' Magnifying Glass

John 17:20-26, v. 20

"I do not pray for these only, but also for those who are to believe in me through their word."

Object: A magnifying glass.

Good morning, boys and girls. How many of you have ever worked or played with a magnifying glass? [*Let them answer.*] A lot of you! I brought one along with me so that we could look through one and see how helpful it is for seeing something that would be hard to see without it. [*Take out the magnifying glass and read some very small print or look at the particles that make up a page of paper.*] Isn't that something, that a piece of glass can help us see so much that we might miss if we did not use it? For some people a magnifying glass is really important in their work. I know that jewelers use them to work on watches, and doctors use them in some operations. Other people find them just as important.

A magnifying glass is something that you look through to see something else. A disciple of Jesus is like a magnifying glass. Did you know that? [*Let them answer.*] That's right, a disciple is someone who helps us to see God a lot better than we can see, and believe, without him. Let's think about Peter or Paul, or any of the other disciples, and remember how much we have learned about Jesus and the teachings of God because of the way that they were and what they said. Jesus knew how important they were, and one of his very last prayers that he said on earth was a prayer for his disciples, saying how thankful he was for those who helped others believe in God. Jesus was telling us that he knew that his disciples were like magnifying glasses for other people, and that they helped the people in Jerusalem and other cities believe in the true God.

You can be a magnifying glass for Jesus also. When you

tell your friends how much you love Jesus, and why you love him, you are being a magnifying glass. That's right; and when you do this you are just like Peter or Paul, or any other disciple. You can tell people how God loves you, forgives you, and makes a place in heaven for you to share with him at just the right time. Did you ever think that someone would call you a magnifying glass? [*Let them answer.*] You are, every time that you show someone else Jesus and what he means to you.

The next time you see a magnifying glass, I hope that you will remember what we said today, and that you will always be a disciple of Jesus Christ.

Are You Who You Say You Are?

John 20:19-31, v. 25

So the other disciples told him, "We have seen the Lord."
But he said to them, "Unless I see in his hands the print of
the nails, and place my finger in the mark of the nails, and
place my hand in his side, I will not believe."

Object: *A driver's license, Social Security card, or an identification bracelet.*

Good morning, boys and girls. How many of you know who you are? [*Let them answer.*] If I asked each of you that question, could you prove to me who you are? [*Let them answer.*] How can you prove that you are who you say you are? [*Let them answer.*] Do you have a piece of paper, or are you wearing something that proves that you are who you say you are? [*Let them answer.*]

If you asked me to prove to you that I am who I say I am, I might give you my driver's license, or my Social Security card. [*Take out your billfold and show them some of your identification.*] There are lots of times when I am asked to prove that I am who I say that I am. People in the banks and stores want to know that I am who I say I am before they will let me cash a check or charge something.

But I want you to know that I am not the only person who has to prove that I am who I say that I am. Did you know that Jesus had to prove to one of his disciples that he was Jesus? [*Let them answer.*] He did. But Jesus did not have a driver's license, and he did not have a Social Security card. If he had something like this, he might have used it, but I doubt that he did.

Let me tell you a story. You will remember that Jesus had been crucified on the cross, and that he had died. When he was crucified, the people drove nails through his hands and his feet into the cross of wood. As you can imagine, it not only hurt a lot, but it also left big holes and scars where the nails went through his skin. It was after Jesus had died and was also resurrected that he had to prove himself. Jesus had visited with all of the disciples except one called Thomas. He had told them how much he loved them and what he was going to do for them. They could hardly wait to tell Thomas about Jesus being with them. But Thomas could not believe that someone who had died could come back to life and visit again. So he told the disciples that unless he saw the places where the nails went through Jesus' hands and feet, he would not believe their story. It was almost a week later when Thomas was with the other disciples that Jesus came again. He knew that Thomas did not believe, so he showed him the marks and scars in his hands and in his side. Then he asked Thomas if he believed. Of couse Thomas did, and that is the day that Jesus proved who he was to many. We can't see those nails, but we must believe what happened to Thomas and to others like him. That is why we call our kind of believing "faith." The next time that you see someone prove who they are with a driver's license, you can remember the day that Jesus proved who he was with the marks of the nails in his body.

The Day Jesus Cooked

*When they got out on land, they saw a charcoal fire there,
with fish lying on it, and bread.*

Object: *Some charcoal and a loaf of bread.*

Good morning, boys and girls. How many of you ever
thought about Jesus cooking breakfast? [*Let them answer.*]
Did you think that Jesus could cook? [*Let them answer.*] You
probably knew that he was a carpenter, but there are not many
places in the Bible that tell you about Jesus as a cook. I don't
know how often he cooked, but the Bible tells of one time that
he did, and it was one of the most exciting events in the Bible.

First of all, you have to know that Jesus had been dead
and had come back to life. This story happened during one
of the times that Jesus visited with his disciples after he was
risen from the dead. As you can imagine, the disciples were
lonely without him, and some of them had decided that they
would go fishing rather than just sit around and think about
the good times they used to have with Jesus. They fished all
night and did not catch anything, but I guess they really did
not care about catching fish. Then, as it became morning, they
saw a man on the beach waving to them and asking them how
they had done with their fishing. Some of them thought right
away that it might be Jesus, but they were not sure. He told
them to put their nets down on the other side of the boat to
catch some fish. They told the man on the beach that they had
fished all night, but that they would cast their nets once more
the way he told them to. As you might guess, they caught more
fish than the nets could hold. Peter knew by now that the man
was Jesus. He jumped into the water and swam ashore. The
others followed him in the boat, and when they got there, they
saw that Jesus had already started a fire with some charcoal

and had some bread ready for them to eat. [*Show them the charcoal and the loaf of bread.*] It may not have looked like my charcoal or my loaf of bread, but it cooked and tasted pretty much the same.

I suppose you can imagine how glad they were to see Jesus. They were thrilled to share breakfast and tell stories about all of the good times they had spent together. Most of all they were glad because they knew once more that Jesus was alive and well, and that he remembered them as people whom he loved and cared for every day, whether he was eating or walking with them. Jesus is that way with us today. He doesn't have to cook for us to show us that he cares for us. We know it anyway, but for the disciples, who had spent so much time with him on earth, it was one of the best things that ever happened to them. Maybe the next time that you have a cookout and you put the charcoal on the fire, you will remember the day that Jesus cooked breakfast for his disciples, and shared some bread and fish with them. I hope you remember it, because it was one of the best moments in the disciples' lives.